Congressional
Research
Service

Congressional Responses to Selected Work Stoppages in Professional Sports

L. Elaine Halchin, Coordinator
Specialist in American National Government

Justin Murray
Information Research Specialist

Jon O. Shimabukuro
Legislative Attorney

Kathleen Ann Ruane
Legislative Attorney

September 17, 2012

Congressional Research Service

7-5700

www.crs.gov

R41060

CRS Report for Congress ——————————————————————

Prepared for Members and Committees of Congress

Summary

Prior to the 2011 National Football League (NFL) lockout, developments in professional football's labor-management relations had prompted questions regarding how, when, and in what manner a new collective bargaining agreement (CBA) might be drafted. Interest in this matter included, on the part of some observers, questions about how Congress responded to previous work stoppages in professional sports. In attempting to address this particular question, this report examines congressional responses to the 1982 and 1987 work stoppages in the NFL. With the conclusion of the 2011 NFL lockout in July, this work stoppage is also included. Additionally, this report examines the 1994 Major League Baseball strike, which is useful considering the extent of congressional activity surrounding this strike.

Compared to the 1994 baseball strike, the 1982 and 1987 football strikes and the 2011 lockout did not garner much attention from Congress in terms of legislative measures and hearings. Three legislative measures were introduced in response to the 1982 strike; one each was introduced in response to the 1987 strike and the 2011 lockout. Members introduced or offered 22 legislative measures and held five hearings that were related to the baseball strike. With one exception (S.Res. 294, 100th Congress), none of these measures was approved by either house.

Members who introduced, or otherwise supported, legislative measures offered reasons for promoting congressional intervention. Their arguments touched on, for example, the economic impact of work stoppages, the role of baseball's antitrust exemption in establishing a climate conducive to players' strikes, previous congressional involvement in professional sports, and a responsibility to ensure the continuity of football (or baseball).

Disagreeing that congressional intervention was warranted, other Members offered several reasons why Congress ought not to intervene. For example, one Member suggested that repealing baseball's antitrust exemption would alter the balance of power in professional baseball. Other Members believed that more pressing matters deserved Congress's attention. At least one Member suggested that a particular bill, if enacted, would have the effect of favoring the players over the owners.

A summary of NFL labor-management history may be found in **Appendix A**. **Appendix B** provides an overview of key aspects of labor-management relations and sports, and **Appendix C** includes a discussion of antitrust exemptions applicable to professional sports.

Contents

Introduction..1
    Work Stoppages in Selected Professional Sports Leagues 1
1982 National Football League Strike 3
    Congressional Response...4
        H.Res. 597 and H.Res. 598 (97th Congress)...4
        S. 3003, Organized Professional Team Sports Labor Dispute Resolution Act of
           1982 (97th Congress) 4
1987 National Football League Strike 5
    Congressional Response...5
1994 Major League Baseball Strike..8
    Congressional Response...8
        S. 2380, H.R. 4965, and S.Amdt. 2601 to H.R. 4649, Baseball Fans Protection
           Act of 1994 (103rd Congress) 12
        S. 2401, National Commission on Major League Baseball Act of 1994 (103rd
           Congress) 13
        H.R. 4994, Baseball Fans and Communities Protection Act of 1994 (103rd
           Congress) 14
        H.R. 5095, Major League Play Ball Act (103rd Congress)... 15
        Hearing on Baseball's Antitrust Exemption and the Strike (103rd Congress) 18
        H.R. 45, Baseball Fans and Communities Protection Act of 1995 (104th Congress)........ 20
        H.R. 105, H.R. 106, H.R. 365, and H.R. 1612 (104th Congress)....................................... 20
        H.R. 120, Baseball Fans and Communities Protection Act of 1995 (104th
           Congress) 20
        H.R. 386, Professional Baseball Antitrust Reform Act of 1995 (104th Congress) 20
        H.R. 397, Major League Play Ball Act (104th Congress)... 20
        H.R. 735, National Commission on Professional Baseball Act of 1995 (104th
           Congress) 21
        H.R. 749 (104th Congress)... 21
        H.R. 870 and S. 376, Major League Baseball Restoration Act (104th Congress).............. 22
        S. 15, National Pastime Preservation Act of 1995 (104th Congress) 22
        S. 415, Professional Baseball Antitrust Reform Act of 1995, and S. 416, Major
           League Baseball Antitrust Reform Act of 1995 (104th Congress)................................. 23
        S. 627, Major League Baseball Antitrust Reform Act of 1995 (104th Congress).............. 26
    White House Efforts to Aid in Resolving the Strike... 27
2011 National Football League Lockout 28
    Congressional Response... 29
Discussion.. 30

Tables

Table 1. MLB Work Stoppages 1
Table 2. NBA Work Stoppages 2
Table 3. NFL Work Stoppages 2

Table 4. NHL Work Stoppages 2

Table 5. 97th Congress: Legislative Measures Related to the 1982 NFL Strike 4

Table 6. 100th Congress: Legislative Measure Related to the 1987 NFL Strike 6

Table 7. 103rd and 104th Congresses: Legislative Measures and Hearing Related to the 1994 MLB Strike 8

Table 8. 112th Congress: Legislative Measure Related to the 2011 NFL Lockout 30

Table 9. Congressional Activity During Strikes... 30

Table 10. Methods Proposed for Resolving the Strikes 32

Table 11. Disposition of Legislative Measures 33

Appendixes

Appendix A. Summary of NFL Labor History 35

Appendix B. Sports and Labor-Management Relations 36

Appendix C. Antitrust Exemptions Applicable to Professional Sports 38

Contacts

Author Contact Information... 42

Introduction

Initially, this report was written in anticipation of a possible strike by National Football League (NFL) players, or a possible lockout by the NFL, in 2011. At that time, developments in professional football's labor-management relations had prompted questions regarding how, when, and in what manner a new collective bargaining agreement (CBA) might be drafted. Interest in this matter included, on the part of some observers, questions about how Congress responded to previous work stoppages in professional sports.

This report examines congressional activity related to the three most recent National Football League (NFL) work stoppages, which occurred in 1982, 1987, and 2011, and the 1994 Major League Baseball (MLB) strike. Although the latter strike involved another professional sports league, it is potentially instructive given the extent of congressional activity surrounding the 1994 strike.

Work Stoppages in Selected Professional Sports Leagues

Work stoppages involving professional sports, whether caused by the players going on strike or the owners imposing a lockout, are by their very nature contentious and not always resolved quickly or easily. Through mid-2012, the four major professional sports leagues in the United States—Major League Baseball (MLB), National Basketball Association (NBA), National Football League, and National Hockey League (NHL)—had experienced a total of 21 work stoppages. **Table 1**, **Table 2**, **Table 3**, and **Table 4** list the work stoppages for each sport.

Table 1. MLB Work Stoppages

Year(s)	Type of Work Stoppage	Duration
1972	Strike	13 days
1973	Lockout	17 days
1976	Lockout	17 days
1980	Strike	8 days
1981	Strike	50 days
1985	Strike	2 days
1990	Lockout	32 days
1994-1995	Strike	232 days

Sources: Major League Baseball, "Collective Bargaining, Labor Timeline," at http://mlb.mlb.com/mlb/news/labor/y2006/index.jsp?content=timeline; Associated Press, "Labor Relations; Fehr: Atmosphere Not As 'Poisoned'" As in 1994," *CNNSI.com*, February 25, 2001, at http://sportsillustrated.cnn.com/baseball/mlb/news/2001/02/25/fehr_labor_ap/; "Labor Matters: Unions," *The Business of Sports*, ed. Scott R. Rosner and Kenneth L. Shropshire (Boston: Jones and Bartlett, 2004), p. 200.

Notes: The Major League Baseball Players Association (MLBPA) became a labor union in 1966. (Major League Baseball Players Association, "MLBPA Info: Frequently Asked Questions," at http://mlbplayers.mlb.com/pa/info/faq.jsp#created.) The current CBA expires on December 11, 2011. (Major League Baseball Players Association, "MLBPA Info: Basic Agreement," at http://mlbplayers.mlb.com/pa/info/cba.jsp.)

Table 2. NBA Work Stoppages

Year(s)	Type of Work Stoppage	Duration
1995	Lockout	77 days
1998-1999	Lockout	191 days
2011	Lockout	149 days

Source: "Labor Matters: Unions," *The Business of Sports*, ed. Scott R. Rosner and Kenneth L. Shropshire (Boston: Jones and Bartlett, 2004), p. 200.

Notes: The National Basketball Players Association (NBPA) was established in 1954. (National Basketball Players' Association, "NBPA History," at http://www.nbpa.com/history.php.) The current CBA "runs through the 2010-11 season." (David Aldridge, "Several Issues Will Come to Head During the NBA Labor Talks," August 4, 2009, at http://www.nba.com/2009/news/features/david_aldridge/08/04/aldridge.labor/index.html.)

Table 3. NFL Work Stoppages

Year(s)	Type of Work Stoppage	Duration
1968	Lockout followed by a strike	10 days
1970	Lockout followed by a strike	20 days
1974	Strike	42 days
1982	Strike	57 days
1987	Strike	24 days
2011	Lockout	135 days

Sources: Paul D. Staudohar, *Playing for Dollars: Labor Relations and the Sports Business*, 3rd ed. (Ithaca, NY: Cornell University Press, 1996), pp. 71-72; Associated Press, "N.F.L. Players Back on Jobs," *New York Times*, October 20,1987, at https://w3.nexis.com, p. B8; William C. Rhoden, "Jets Roar Past Patriots as Season Comes to a Pause," *New York Times*, September 22, 1987, at https://w3.nexis.com, p. A29; NFL Players Association, "History, The 1970's – AFL and NFL Players Associations Merge," at http://www.nflplayers.com/user/template.aspx?fmid=182&lmid=239&pid=1036&type=c; NFL Players Association, "History, The 1960's – ALF/NFL Competition," at http://www.nflplayers.com/user/template.aspx?fmid=182&lmid=239&pid=1033&type=c; "Labor Matters: Unions," *The Business of Sports*, ed. Scott R. Rosner and Kenneth L. Shropshire (Boston: Jones and Bartlett2004), p. 200.

Notes: The NFL Players Association (NFLPA) was established in 1956. (NFL Players Association, "History, The Beginning – 1956," at http://nflplayers.com/user/template.aspx?fmid=182&lmid=239&pid=1915&type=c.) However, it was not until 1970 that the AFL Players Association and the NFL Players Association merged, retaining the name of the latter and becoming a recognized union. (NFL Players Association, "History, The 1970's – AFL and NFL Players Associations Merge," at http://nflplayers.com/user/template.aspx?fmid=182&lmid=239&pid=1036&type=c.)

Table 4. NHL Work Stoppages

Year(s)	Type of Work Stoppage	Duration
1992	Strike	10 days
1994-1995	Lockout	103 days
2004-2005	Lockout	302 days
2012	Lockout	In progress[a]

Sources: Paul D. Staudohar, *Playing for Dollars: Labor Relations and the Sports Business*, 3rd ed. (Ithaca, NY: Cornell University Press, 1996), p. 151; Associated Press, "NHL Lockout Chronology," February 16, 2005, at http://sports.espn.go.com/nhl/news/story?id=1993004; Joe LaPointe, "Play Hockey! Settlement Ends 10-Day Strike," *New York Times*, April 11, 1992, at http://www.nytimes.com/1992/04/11/sports/hockey-play-hockey-settlement-ends-10-day-strike.html?scp=46&sq=Bob+Goodenow&st=nyt; Associated Press, "NHL Lockout Chronology," *USAToday.com*, July 13, 2005, at http://www.usatoday.com/sports/hockey/nhl/2005-07-13-lockout-chronology_x.htm; "Labor Matters: Unions," *The Business of Sports*, ed. Scott R. Rosner and Kenneth L. Shropshire (Boston: Jones and Bartlett2004), p. 200.

Notes: The National Hockey League Players' Association was established in 1967. (National Hockey League Players' Association, "What Is the NHLPA?" at http://www.nhlpa.com/AboutTheNHLPA/WhatIs.asp.)

a. At 12:05 am, September 16, 2012, the NHL announced that a deadline had passed on September 15 for the league and the National Hockey League Players' Association (NHLPA) to agree on a new CBA. (National Hockey League, "CBA Expires With No Agreement Reached," news release, September 16, 2012, at http://www.nhl.com/ice/news.htm?id=641628.)

Major League Baseball has experienced the greatest number of work stoppages (eight), followed by the NFL (five), NHL (four), and NBA (two). While both NBA work stoppages were lockouts, the other three leagues have experienced a combination of strikes and lockouts. Major League Baseball has had five strikes and three lockouts, and the NHL one strike and three lockouts. The NFL is somewhat unusual in that two of its five work stoppages began as lockouts and concluded as strikes (1968 and 1970). The average length of work stoppages for each league is as follows: MLB, 46 days (excluding the 232-day strike, the average is 20 days); NBA, 139 days; NFL, 31 days; and NHL, 138 days (excluding the 10-day strike, the average is 203 days).[1] The medians for the four leagues are as follows: MLB, 17 days; NBA, 149 days; NFL, 24 days; and NHL, 103 days.[2]

In the following three sections, this report describes congressional responses to the 1982 and 1987 NFL strikes and the 1994 MLB strike, respectively. The latter section also includes a discussion of the Clinton Administration's attempts to facilitate the resolution of the baseball strike. A summary of the circumstances of each strike is followed by a table that identifies relevant legislative measures, and an overview of Members' comments and report language regarding the strike, which were drawn from congressional hearings and reports, and remarks made on the House or Senate floor. This information shows the extent of actual, or intended, congressional involvement and how some Members viewed congressional involvement in the strike. A summary of NFL labor-management history may be found in **Appendix A**. **Appendix B** provides an overview of key aspects of labor-management relations and sports, and **Appendix C** includes a discussion of antitrust exemptions applicable to professional sports.

1982 National Football League Strike

On September 20, 1982, NFL players voted to strike after negotiations for a new collective bargaining agreement broke down. The previous CBA had expired on July 15, 1982. Initially, the NFL Players Association (NFLPA) sought 55% of the owners' gross revenues. The NFL rejected the players association's demands and offered to share $1.6 billion with the NFLPA over five years. The dispute was resolved when the players association accepted the owners' offer to share $1.28 billion over five years and to provide $60 million to the union to compensate players for salaries not paid during the strike. The season resumed on November 21, 1982. On December 5, 1982, the players association and the owners signed a new five-year CBA. After the strike was

---

[1] Averages were rounded.

[2] The figures for the NHL exclude the work stoppage that began in September 2012 because it is in progress.

resolved, the season resumed with a seven-game regular season schedule and an expanded playoff bracket, which culminated in Super Bowl XVI on January 30, 1983.[3]

Congressional Response

Table 5 shows the legislative measures that were introduced in response to the strike.

Table 5. 97th Congress: Legislative Measures Related to the 1982 NFL Strike

Legislative Measure (Congress)	Brief Summary	Hearing Held or Written Report Published?	Number of Cosponsors	Final Major Action
H.Res. 597 (97th)	Support a prompt settlement of the NFL strike.	No	0	House Committee on Education and Labor referred the bill to the Subcommittee on Labor-Management Relations.
H.Res. 598 (97th)	Support a prompt settlement of the NFL strike.	No	14	House Committee on Education and Labor referred the bill to the Subcommittee on Labor-Management Relations.
S. 3003 (97th)	Establish a final offer arbitration procedure for labor disputes involving professional baseball, basketball, football, and hockey.[a]	No	0	Senate Committee on Labor and Human Resources referred the bill to the Subcommittee on Labor and requested comment from the Department of Labor and the Office of Management and Budget.

Source: Legislative Information System, at http://www.congress.gov.

Note:

a.   This bill also would have required the parties to the current NFL strike "to resume activities" and authorized the President to direct them to submit final offers in accordance with Sec. 2 of S. 3003 within five days of the date of enactment.

H.Res. 597 and H.Res. 598[4] (97th Congress)

Either resolution, if passed, would have urged the parties to take steps to promptly settle the strike and resume the season.

S. 3003, Organized Professional Team Sports Labor Dispute Resolution Act of 1982 (97th Congress)

Although no hearings were held, the bill's sponsor, Senator Ted Stevens, offered a rationale for congressional involvement when he introduced S. 3003. Noting that "Congress has clearly

---

[3] The 1982 strike was the first regular-season strike in the then 63-year history of the National Football League. Two previous "pre-season actions" occurred in 1970 and 1974 but did not extend beyond the start of the regular season.

[4] According to the Legislative Information System, neither resolution had a short title.

---

established a history of promoting the public interest in professional sports," he then mentioned several instances when legislation involving professional sports was enacted:[5]

> For example, in 1973, we adopted legislation calling for the telecasting of sold-out home games of professional sports teams. We also enacted legislation encouraging the stability of professional sports leagues by confirming, in 1961, the right of professional sport leagues to jointly sell their television rights to the national networks. In 1966, we authorized the consolidation of the American Football League and the National Football League so that football franchises could continue to operate on a stable basis in their resident communities. Thus we have long recognized the public interest in encouraging professional sports, and have affirmatively acted to encourage the financial stability of the leagues.[6]

Senator Stevens also noted the adverse economic consequences of the football strike, mentioning that the "strike produced major economic disruptions and losses in all of the communities which host NFL teams."[7]

1987 National Football League Strike

The 1982 CBA expired on August 31, 1987, and shortly thereafter negotiations broke down between the NFLPA and the NFL over the issue of free agency and other matters. The union voted to strike on September 22, 1987. The owners cancelled the games scheduled for September 26 and September 27, 1987, while announcing their intention to resume the season on October 4, 1987, with replacement players. NFL players who did not share the union's concerns regarding free agency, or who needed the money, played alongside the replacement players.[8]

The striking players voted to return to work on October 15, 1987, even though there was no CBA. Team owners, however, banned players who had not agreed to return to work by the owner-imposed deadline of October 14, 1987, from participating in that week's scheduled games. Thus, striking players who did not return to their teams until after the NFLPA vote lost an additional week of pay. Replacement players were released as the regular players returned to their jobs. The 1987-1988 season concluded on January 31, 1988, when the Super Bowl was held at Jack Murphy Stadium in San Diego.

Congressional Response

Table 6 shows the legislative measure that was introduced in response to the strike.

---

[5] Sen. Ted Stevens, "Professional Football Strike," remarks in the Senate, *Congressional Record*, vol. 128, part 17 (October 1, 1982), p. 26731.

[6] Ibid.

[7] Ibid., p. 26730.

[8] NFL Players Association, "A Strike vs. A Lockout," March 16, 2008, at http://nflplayers.com/user/content.aspx?fmid=178&lmid=443&pid=412&type=n&weigh=443,0,412,n.

Table 6. 100th Congress: Legislative Measure Related to the 1987 NFL Strike

Legislative Measure (Congress)	Brief Summary	Hearing Held or Written Report Published?	Number of Cosponsors	Final Major Action
S.Res. 294 (100th)	Support a prompt settlement of the NFL strike.	No	2	Agreed to by voice vote.

Source: Legislative Information System, at http://www.congress.gov.

S.Res. 294, which was agreed to without amendment by a voice vote, called on both parties—the players association and the NFL Management Council—to resume negotiations.[9]

Although S.Res. 291 (100th Congress), which addressed the telecasting practices of the NFL, was not a response to the NFL players' strike, the subject was broached during a hearing on the resolution.[10] Following his introduction of Pete Rozelle, then-commissioner of the NFL, the subcommittee's chairman initiated the following exchange with Rozelle regarding the ongoing strike:

> Senator METZENBAUM. Mr. Rozelle, as I indicated to you before the hearing, I think for us to have you before this hearing and not inquire of you as to why you as the Commissioner have not been heard from in connection with some effort to settle the strike between the players and the NFL, would be surprising to the many people in this country that are asking that question. I wonder if you would be good enough to tell us why you as the Commissioner have not seen fit to move in and at least attempt to mediate the issue.
>
> Mr. ROZELLE. I have had meetings with the President of the Players' Association, Gene Upshaw, and phone conversations. I have attempted to stay close to the situation, of course, on the owners' Management Council side. There has been a very, very strong disagreement on several issues that have inhibited the negotiating process. I am pleased now that I think that perhaps certain pressures are involved on both sides, and I understand they are going to be meeting promptly to get back into negotiating. I think it is unfortunate they could not have accomplished more back in May, June and July, but it was all the thrust at once when the season came on us.
>
> Senate METZENBAUM. Well, I might say I think that all of us are pleased to know that management and players are going back to the negotiating table. I never heard of a strike that was settled without direct negotiations, oftentimes through some mediator—whether it is

---

[9] Sen. Robert Dole, "Senate Resolution (S.Res. 294)—Calling for An End to the 10-Day-Old Pro Football Strike," remarks in the Senate, *Congressional Record*, vol. 133, part 19 (October 1, 1987), p. 26146. According to the Legislative Information System, this resolution did not have a short title.

[10] Sen. Arlen Specter's rationale for S.Res. 291 was as follows: "In 1961, at the request of the NFL, Congress enacted the Sports Broadcasting Act (15 U.S.C. §§1291-95), which granted antitrust immunity to the NFL's pooling of revenues from sponsored television broadcasts. This permitted the NFL to enter into a series of leaguewide network television contracts.... At no time since the original grant of limited immunity 26 years ago, however, has the Department of Justice reviewed the NFL's telecasting practices to determine whether they are in compliance with the law. Since the law's enactment, there have been dramatic changes in the nature of telecommunications and in the NFL's telecasting practices.... Mr. President, I long have been concerned about the possibility that the NFL might remove a portion of its televised games from free broadcast television, available to the public at no charge, and offer them instead only to fans who can afford to pay—whether for cable service or on a 'pay-per-view' basis." (Sen. Arlen Specter, "Report on National Football League Telecasting," remarks in the Senate, *Congressional Record*, vol. 133, part 18 (September 29, 1987), p. 25637.)

---

from the U.S. Mediation and Conciliation Service or someone else.... The American people have a strong interest in this issue. They do not have an ownership right, but they feel they have some type of right in professional football. And I think the sooner the matter gets resolved and the parties themselves meet together and resolve it, I think the happier the American people will be. I think it will be one less issue to be on the top of the news in the nightly news every night.[11]

In an exchange that occurred later in the hearing, Senator Arlen Specter similarly encouraged the NFL commissioner to assist in settling the strike. The relevant excerpt is as follows:

Senator SPECTER. Okay. I would like to disagree with Senator Hatch, even though he is gone, on one small point. That is about the adequacy of the substitute games on this past Sunday. I would join my colleague, Senator Metzenbaum, Commissioner Rozelle, in urging you to do everything you could personally to lend your good offices to settle the strike. You have been a very powerful force in the National Football League for many, many years. I believe you became Commissioner in the 1950s.

Mr. ROZELLE. 1960, Senator.

Senator SPECTER. 1960. Okay. But you have been the Commissioner for 27 years, one of the toughest jobs around, pulled together the National Football League in an era of extraordinary growth and extraordinary complexity, and you have appeared before this Judiciary Committee on many occasions in my short tenure in the United States Senate. I think you have always done a very able job, and I think you have done a very able job here this morning. I would very much like to see your talents used this afternoon to settle the football strike.

Mr. ROZELLE. I would love to, believe me. It is so terribly frustrating, Senator.

Mr. MODELL. I would like to add a thought in that regard. Yes, I echo your sentiments on what he has done for 26, 27 years. But if the players were to accept him as a neutral Commissioner, which he really is, this strike never would have gotten off the ground. They view him as an owners' appointee, and that gives us great difficulty.[12]

Senator SPECTER. Well, the strike has gotten off the ground, but I think it is a little different ball game today than it was a week ago. We have had a week of substitute players. I think the American public is totally dissatisfied with that. There have been incidents around the league which are not a credit for anybody. And I think it is time it came to a close. If there is one man who could probably do it better than anyone else, if anybody could do it, it is Commissioner Rozelle. So we are going to let you go early, Commissioner.[13]

---

[11] U.S. Congress, Senate Judiciary, Antitrust, Monopolies and Business Rights, *Antitrust Implications of the Recent NFL Television Contract*, hearing on S.Res. 291, 100th Cong., 1st sess., October 6, 1987, S.Hrg. 100-919 (Washington: GPO, 1988), p. 11. (Capitalization in original.)

[12] Arthur B. Modell was the president of the Cleveland Browns. He accompanied Mr. Rozelle.

[13] U.S. Congress, Senate Judiciary, Antitrust, Monopolies and Business Rights, *Antitrust Implications of the Recent NFL Television Contract*, p. 36. (Capitalization in original.)

1994 Major League Baseball Strike

Unable to reach an agreement with the owners on a new CBA in summer 1994, major league players voted, on August 12, 1994, to strike. Approximately one month later, on September 14, 1994, Major League Baseball cancelled the remainder of the season. The decisions to strike and to cancel the season followed several months of negotiations over a number of issues, including baseball's revenue sharing plan. Beginning in fall 1994, the Clinton Administration attempted to facilitate negotiations between the parties.[14] The work stoppage ended in early 1995 following then-U.S. District Court Judge Sonia Sotomayor's issuance of an injunction that had been "requested by the National Labor Relations Board ordering baseball owners to restore bidding on free agents, a resumption and salary arbitration and the anti-collusion rules which were a part" of the CBA that had expired the previous year.[15] Shortly after Judge Sotomayor issued the injunction, which occurred on March 31, 1995, major league baseball owners "accepted the players' offer to return to work."[16] Although the commencement of the 1995 season was delayed, beginning on April 26 instead of April 3, which was the original opening day, the season was played without interruption and the postseason concluded with the World Series.[17]

Congressional Response

Table 7 shows the legislative measures that were introduced in response to the strike.

Table 7. 103rd and 104th Congresses: Legislative Measures and Hearing Related to the 1994 MLB Strike

Legislative Measure or Hearing (Congress)	Brief Summary	Hearing Held or Written Report Published?	Number of Cosponsors	Final Major Action
S. 2380 (103rd)a	Apply antitrust laws to a term or condition unilaterally imposed by any party to the MLB CBA.	No	3	Placed on the Senate Legislative Calendar under General Orders.
S.Amdt. 2601 to H.R. 4649 (103rd)	Apply antitrust laws to a term or condition unilaterally imposed by any party to the MLB CBA.	No	1	Withdrawn in the Senate.

[14] See "White House Efforts to Aid in Resolving the Strike" for additional information.

[15] Ted Keith, "Supreme Court Nominee Sonia Sotomayor Well Known in Sports," *SI.com*, May 26, 2009, at http://sportsillustrated.cnn.com/2009/baseball/mlb/05/26/sotomayor/index.html.

[16] Murray Chass, "Baseball Owners Quit Fight; Opening Day Is Set for April 26," *New York Times*, April 3, 1995, at http://www.lexis.com.

[17] Ibid.

Legislative Measure or Hearing (Congress)	Brief Summary	Hearing Held or Written Report Published?	Number of Cosponsors	Final Major Action
H.R. 4965 (103rd)[a]	Apply antitrust laws to a term or condition unilaterally imposed by any party to the MLB CBA.	No	0	House Committee on the Judiciary referred the bill to the Subcommittee on Economic and Commercial Law.
S. 2401 (103rd)	Establish a National Commission on Major League Baseball to oversee and regulate MLB, including the conduct of binding arbitration in the event of a labor impasse.	No	0	Referred to the Senate Committee on Commerce.
H.R. 4994 (103rd)	Apply antitrust laws to term(s) or condition(s) unilaterally imposed by any party to the MLB CBA.	Yes	6	Placed on the Union Calendar.
H.R. 5095 (103rd)	Effective February 1, 1995, establish an arbitration board to conduct binding arbitration for MLB owners and players.	Yes	0	House Committee on Education and Labor requested executive comment from Labor.[b]
House Committee on the Judiciary, Subcommittee on Economic and Commercial Law (103rd)	Major League Baseball's antitrust exemption and its relationship to the ongoing strike.	Yes	Not applicable	Hearing published in 1994.
H.R. 45 (104th)	Apply antitrust laws to a term or condition unilaterally imposed by any party to the MLB CBA.	No	0	Referred to the House Committee on the Judiciary.
H.R. 105 (104th)	Exclude professional baseball from the antitrust exemption applicable to certain television contracts.	No	0	Referred to the House Committee on the Judiciary.
H.R. 106 (104th)	Apply antitrust laws to professional baseball teams and leagues.	No	7	Referred to the House Committee on the Judiciary.

Legislative Measure or Hearing (Congress)	Brief Summary	Hearing Held or Written Report Published?	Number of Cosponsors	Final Major Action
H.R. 120 (104th)	Apply antitrust laws to term(s) or condition(s) unilaterally imposed by any party to the MLB CBA.	No	9	Referred to the House Committee on the Judiciary.
H.R. 365 (104th)	Apply antitrust laws to term(s) or condition(s) unilaterally imposed by any party to the MLB CBA.	No	0	Referred to the House Committee on the Judiciary.
H.R. 386 (104th)	Apply antitrust laws to professional baseball.	No	3	Referred to the House Committee on the Judiciary.
H.R. 397 (104th)	Effective February 1, 1995, establish an arbitration board to conduct binding arbitration for MLB owners and players.	No	0	House Committee on Economic and Educational Opportunities referred the bill to the Subcommittee on Employer-Employee Relations.
H.R. 735 (104th)	Establish a National Commission on Professional Baseball to oversee and investigate major league and minor league baseball, including the conduct of binding arbitration in the event of a labor impasse between MLB and players.	No	0	Referred to the House Committee on the Judiciary. Referred by the House Committee on Commerce to the Subcommittee on Commerce, Trade, and Hazardous Materials. Referred by the House Committee on Economic and Educational Opportunities to the Subcommittee on Employer-Employee Relations.
H.R. 749 (104th)	Apply antitrust laws to professional baseball teams and leagues.	No	0	Referred to the House Committee on the Judiciary.

Legislative Measure or Hearing (Congress)	Brief Summary	Hearing Held or Written Report Published?	Number of Cosponsors	Final Major Action
H.R. 870 (104th)c	Establish a National Baseball Dispute Resolution Panel, which shall resolve the current labor dispute by setting forth a binding agreement.	No	6	House Committee on Economic and Educational Opportunities referred the bill to the Subcommittee on Employer-Employee Relations.
H.R. 1612 (104th)	Apply antitrust laws to professional baseball.	No	6	Referred to the House Committee on the Judiciary.
S. 15 (104th)	Except as provided in P.L. 87-331 (Sports Broadcasting Act of 1961), apply antitrust laws to professional baseball.	No	2	Referred to the Senate Committee on the Judiciary.
S. 376 (104th)c	Establish a National Baseball Dispute Resolution Panel, which shall resolve the current labor dispute by setting forth a binding agreement.	No	1	Placed on Senate Legislative Calendar under General Orders.
S. 415 (104th)	Apply antitrust laws to professional baseball's labor relations.	Yesd	4	Hearing held by the Senate Committee on the Judiciary, Subcommittee on Antitrust and Business.
S. 416 (104th)	Apply antitrust laws to professional major league baseball.	Yesd	1	Hearing held by the Senate Committee on the Judiciary, Subcommittee on Antitrust and Business.
S. 627 (104th)	Apply antitrust laws to professional major league baseball.	Yes	4	Placed on Senate Legislative Calendar under General Orders.

Source: Legislative Information System, at http://www.congress.gov.

Notes:

a.   S. 2380 and H.R. 4965 were companion bills.

b.   This appears to be a reference to the Department of Labor.

c.   H.R. 870 and S. 376 were companion bills.

d.   One hearing was held for S. 415 and S. 416.

S. 2380, H.R. 4965, and S.Amdt. 2601 to H.R. 4649, Baseball Fans Protection Act of 1994 (103rd Congress)

Senator Howard Metzenbaum introduced S. 2380 and offered S.Amdt. 2601. H.R. 4649 was a companion bill to S. 2380.

Senator Metzenbaum believed that "revoking the owners' antitrust immunity is the best long-term solution to the mess the players and the owners have made of major league baseball," but he decided to offer instead what he characterized as a "compromise bill."[18] He went on to explain his reasoning as follows:

> It [S. 2380] does not eliminate the players right to strike, or the owners right to lock them out. Instead, the bill allows the antitrust laws to be invoked if the owners impose a salary cap or any other terms and conditions on the players. This should take away the owners' incentive to play hard ball and impose unilateral conditions. It should also relieve players' fear that they need to strike in order to prevent a salary cap from being shoved down their throats when the season ends. Once the owners and players resolve their differences and sign a new agreement, the bill expires....[19]

> Right now, the big league players cannot use the antitrust laws. If they could, the owners would have to deal with them fairly or face the consequences in a court of law. In other words, what this bill does is give the players another tool they can use to avoid striking, or to

[18] Sen. Howard Metzenbaum, "The Baseball Fans Protection Act of 1994," remarks in the Senate, *Congressional Record*, daily edition, August 11, 1994, p. S11342. Although S. 500 (103rd Congress), which was introduced in March 1993 and would have eliminated baseball's antitrust exemption, was not related to the baseball strike, it is mentioned here. Sen. Metzenbaum, upon introducing S. 500, related his perspective, as follows, regarding the exemption and labor relations: "8. How does the exemption affect relations with the players? Up until the mid-1970s, baseball needed the exemption in order to preserve the validity of the reserve clause. The reserve clause bound a player to the team which first signed him for the duration of his baseball career. In essence, the reserve clause was an agreement among the owners not to compete in the market for player services. Generally, such agreements would not pass muster under the antitrust laws. While a portion of major league players (those with more than 6 years experience) can become free agents, the bulk of big leaguers still have no opportunity to offer their services in a free market. Because these restrictions on the mobility of major leaguers are now included in the current collective bargaining agreement with the players, they would not be subject to challenge under the antitrust laws. However, the current labor agreement expires at the end of this year. If the owners and the players fail to reach an agreement, the owners could unilaterally impose restrictions on player mobility that would limit the competition for player services and thus probably run afoul of the antitrust laws. However, because of the exemption, the baseball players—unlike the football or basketball players— would have no ability to challenge the restrictions under the antitrust laws. Their only recourse against unreasonable restrictions on player mobility would be a strike. Thus, the antitrust exemption makes labor negotiations between the owners and the players more confrontational than they might be otherwise. That helps to explain why there has been a work stoppage (either a lockout or a strike) in baseball during every labor negotiation in the last five years.... Removing the exemption ... should foster more stable labor relations. As noted above, the antitrust exemption exacerbates the tendency of the owners and players to be confrontational in labor negotiations. A work stoppage is more likely in baseball than in the other sports because the players have no opportunity to bring an antitrust challenge against the restrictions on their mobility imposed by the owners. The owners have no reason to fear an antitrust suit, so their incentive to compromise is diminished; meanwhile, a strike is the players only option if the owners seek to unreasonably limit competition for player services." (Sen. Howard Metzenbaum, "Professional Baseball Antitrust Reform Act of 1993," remarks in the Senate, *Congressional Record*, daily edition, March 4, 1993, p. S2419.) Two additional bills introduced early in the 103rd Congress, H.R. 108 and H.R. 1549, also sought to apply antitrust laws to major league baseball and remove baseball from the Sports Broadcasting Act of 1961 (15 U.S.C. §§1291-1294), respectively. Since both bills were introduced several months before the commencement of the strike, and the bills' sponsors did not make statements about their measures, it is not known whether the status of labor negotiations were part of the rationale for either bill.

[19] Sen. Howard Metzenbaum, "The Baseball Fans Protection Act of 1994," p. S11342.

bring a strike to a quick end. The last seven times the baseball players and owners have met at the bargaining table there has been a work stoppage: A strike or lockout. This has not happened in other professional sports because those players could use the antitrust laws to settle labor disputes.... If the antitrust laws applied to baseball, the owners could not force the players to accept unreasonable terms and conditions if their labor negotiations hit impasse. The players could challenge the owners unreasonable demands by launching an antitrust suit instead of shutting down the season.[20]

Senator Orrin Hatch, who co-sponsored S. 2380, encouraged both sides to resolve their differences, and, unlike Senator Metzenbaum, did not support the blanket repeal of major league baseball's antitrust immunity.[21] Couching the barriers to resolution as the result of a "legal anomaly," Senator Hatch offered the following explanation of his position:

> On the one hand, professional baseball enjoys a unique and longstanding immunity from the antitrust laws. I have opposed repeal of this immunity, and I continue to do so. On the other hand, the owners retain the right under our current labor laws to impose unilaterally new terms and conditions of employment once an impasse in the bargaining has been reached. I am concerned that the unique combination of these two legal roles, which occurs in no other industry, has the effect of inviting delay and of discouraging prompt resolution of the pending labor dispute. The Baseball Fans Protection Act that Senator Metzenbaum and I are introducing would correct this legal anomaly.[22]

The sponsor of H.R. 4965, Representative Major R. Owens, did not provide any remarks when he introduced his bill.

S. 2401, National Commission on Major League Baseball Act of 1994 (103rd Congress)

Introduced by Senator Dennis DeConcini, S. 2401, if enacted, would have established a commission on professional baseball. Major League Baseball did not have a commissioner at the time of the strike, and Senator DeConcini envisioned the panel serving as an "impartial commissioner" that would "give the fans a much needed voice in the debate."[23] Among the many responsibilities he set forth for the proposed commission, he noted that "[m]ost importantly ... is the Commission's power to conduct binding arbitration of a labor impasse. Given that we are currently in the eighth work stoppage in the past 22 seasons, it is unfortunate, but obvious, that baseball can not put its own house in order."[24] Continuing with the theme that intervention was necessary to resolve the dispute, Senator DeConcini, in the following excerpt, also defended government involving itself in the matter:

> Many people might wonder why, or if, Government should involve itself in this matter. But the Government is already involved and has, in effect, created a baseball monopoly.... This exemption allows baseball to operate as one large entity which operates free of the threat of

---

[20] Ibid.

[21] Sen. Orrin Hatch, "The Baseball Fans Protection Act of 1994," remarks in the Senate, *Congressional Record*, daily edition, August 11, 1994, p. S11343.

[22] Ibid.

[23] Sen. Dennis DeConcini, "National Commission on Major League Baseball Act of 1994," remarks in the Senate, *Congressional Record*, daily edition, August 17, 1994, p. S11994.

[24] Ibid.

competition, despite the fact that competition is the hallmark of American free enterprise. In other instances where we create a monopoly, such as utilities, no one questions the Government's authority to regulate the industry. In essence we grant the monopoly, but we do so with the understanding that this rare exception has conditions, one of which is the Government's right to regulate.[25]

While Senator DeConcini acknowledged that some thought Congress ought to repeal baseball's antitrust exemption, he "[thought] the larger issue [was] ... whether or not the game [could] ... police itself—I have not seen much recently to suggest that it can."[26]

H.R. 4994, Baseball Fans and Communities Protection Act of 1994 (103rd Congress)

Upon introducing H.R. 4994, Representative Mike Synar noted that it was "designed to spur the now stagnant negotiations between the players and owners of major league baseball. This bill is specifically designed to allow the players to get back to the field while all parties to the strike have their rights and bargaining positions protected through the application of the antitrust laws.... [G]iving the players antitrust remedies will preserve their bargaining [position] during the upcoming negotiations without having to resort to a strike."[27]

The committee report that accompanied the bill set forth the same reasoning, as shown by the following excerpt from the report:

> H.R. 4994 would subject Major League Baseball owners and players to the Nation's antitrust laws in the event one of those parties unilaterally imposes an anticompetitive term or condition on the other. While the case for a far broader repeal of the antitrust exemption is compelling, at this late juncture in the 103d Congress, the Committee opted to respond legislatively to the most urgent competitive problem facing Major League Baseball[:] its failure to be subject to the same antitrust rules as the other sports in the event of a breakdown of the collective bargaining process and the unilateral imposition of terms by one of the parties. As such, the legislation was specifically drafted so that it would not implicate issues relating to other activities, such as the operation of the minor leagues or franchise relocation.[28]

> The Committee's formal action of partially repealing the nonstatutory antitrust exemption which Congress never initiated or endorsed but by which it has been saddled for over 70 years is really the first step in ending a legal fiction about the game created and perpetuated by the Supreme Court, as perhaps one of its greatest indulgences. That indulgence, fueled first by sentimentality and then by risk-aversion, has now vested such complete power over the sport by its financial owners as to enable them to end the game at will.[29]

---

[25] Ibid.

[26] Ibid.

[27] Rep. Mike Synar, "Introduction of the Baseball Fans and Communities Protection Act—Hon. Mike Synar," extension of remarks, *Congressional Record*, daily edition, August 18, 1994, p. E1764.

[28] U.S. Congress, House Committee on the Judiciary, *Baseball Fans and Communities Protection Act of 1994*, report to accompany H.R. 4994, 103rd Cong., 2nd sess., November 29, 1994, H.Rept. 103-871 (Washington: GPO, 1994), p. 34.

[29] Ibid., p. 2.

The Committee now acts to end the illusion which has spawned very real economic consequences. It does so by partially repealing the nonstatutory exemption created by the 1922 decision in Federal Baseball Club of Baltimore v. National League of Professional Baseball Clubs. In so doing, the Committee responds to the current phase of a recurring crisis in baseball in a very limited, yet crucial, way: by subjecting the traditional parties to Major League Baseball's collective bargaining agreement the players union and owners to the Nation's antitrust laws in the event one party unilaterally imposes an anticompetitive term or condition of employment on the other.[30]

Other members of the Judiciary Committee disagreed, objecting to, among other things, congressional involvement in the matter. They wrote:

We continue to be concerned about both the propriety and timing of this legislation and oppose its enactment. Simply put, Congress should not intervene in an ongoing collective bargaining dispute unless a national security interest is involved. Clearly, as important as baseball is to our national psyche, a baseball strike is not a national security matter. The decision to legislatively move ahead on this matter at this point is also highly questionable. It would make more sense for Congress to revisit the basic issue of baseball's antitrust exemption next year, when the emotion and acrimony surrounding the current strike hopefully will have subsided.[31]

The dissenting members of the committee also tackled the claim that the antitrust exemption served as a barrier to resolving the ongoing dispute between baseball players and owners. They noted that the other three professional sports leagues (basketball, football, and hockey) did not have the same antitrust exemption that baseball has, yet "all three ... have seen considerable labor strife, not dissimilar to that which we are witnessing with respect to baseball. It would appear that labor strife in professional sports has more to do with economics, than it has to do with the applicability of the federal antitrust laws."[32]

H.R. 5095, Major League Play Ball Act (103rd Congress)

A September 1994 hearing on H.R. 5095 offers some insight into how several members of the House Committee on Education and Labor, Subcommittee on Labor-Management Relations viewed the role of Congress in the strike. The following passages show that the chairman of the subcommittee, Representative Pat Williams, acknowledged, and concurred with, the committee's long-standing opposition to binding arbitration, but then explained why he chose to support congressional intervention in this instance:

I want to tell our witnesses that you are appearing before a committee which has historically opposed binding arbitration. The Labor Committee is the committee that believes that collective bargaining works in America and should be allowed to continue unhampered by Federal intervention. That is my own belief, but this is baseball. However, for this committee to be encouraging binding arbitration is historic and virtually unprecedented.[33]

---

[30] Ibid., pp. 2-3.

[31] Ibid., p. 41.

[32] Ibid., p. 44.

[33] U.S. Congress, House Committee on Education and Labor, Subcommittee on Labor-Management Relations, *The Impact on Collective Bargaining of the Antitrust Exemption*, H.R. 5095, Major League Play Ball Act of 1995, 103rd Cong., 2nd sess., September 29, 1994, Serial No. 103-108 (Washington: GPO, 1995), p. 1.

Representative Williams's comments at the hearing echoed the statement he made upon introducing the bill. An excerpt of the statement is as follows:

> This bill addresses the inability of the owners and players to collectively bargain effectively given the antitrust exemption for baseball.... Collective bargaining in this country works very well. Government should intervene in that process only at times of crises, and then only when it is clear that continued voluntary negotiations will not succeed.[34] My legislation is introduced in that spirit.[35]

Several other subcommittee members followed suit in supporting the use of binding arbitration to settle the strike. Similar to the chairman's approach, each of these other subcommittee members implied or suggested that collective bargaining is preferable, but that binding arbitration, or congressional intervention, is acceptable when parties are unable to reach an agreement.

Excerpts from Representative Donald M. Payne's, Representative Matthew G. Martinez's, and Representative Eliot L. Engel's statements, respectively, are as follows:

> I support the Chairman's initiative because I believe that collective bargaining is a positive tool in this country. The government should step in the picture when it is evident that continued voluntary negotiations are futile. If this bill [H.R. 5095] can alleviate some of the problems that resulted from the baseball strike this summer, then this legislation has my full support.[36] [Payne]
>
> Binding arbitration, I think, is one way to settle these things when there are disputes like that, and while I am a strong labor supporter, I have never really felt that even with labor that there are times when a third party shouldn't step in and see things in a reasonable, objective way when the negotiating parties can't.[37] [Martinez]
>
> I urge the parties to resolve their differences so that congressional intervention is not necessary, but I assure you that we will get involved in order to protect the interests of fans, local business owners, and, as they say, the best interests of baseball.[38] [Engel]

Another subcommittee member who supported this bill, Representative Major R. Owens, believed that the preferable, long-term solution was to repeal baseball's antitrust exemption. In the following excerpt, he provides his reasoning:

> While I fully support this bill, of course, it only provides a temporary solution to a long-term problem. The Congress really must take stronger action. Baseball's antitrust exemption has

---

[34] As demonstrated by the following statement, the subcommittee chairman believed that the parties to the dispute were not able to resolve the dispute themselves: "We have this strike that has more attention than steel strikes, rail strikes, coal strikes, and you are not sitting at the table and talking. It is extraordinarily unusual in American collective bargaining history. Folks just want to get you back to the table. If binding arbitration doesn't do it, okay, if breaking the antitrust thing doesn't do it, okay, you just want to be told to go back, okay, go back. Now. But you know what, that ain't going to get it, not with you guys, it ain't going to get it. You are too far apart. You can't come together."[34] (Ibid., p. 113.)

[35] Rep. Pat Williams, "Play Baseball in 1995," extension of remarks, *Congressional Record*, daily edition, September 23, 1994, p. E1927.

[36] U.S. Congress, House Committee on Education and Labor, Subcommittee on Labor-Management Relations, *The Impact on Collective Bargaining of the Antitrust Exemption*, pp. 9-10.

[37] Ibid., p. 5.

[38] Ibid., p. 8.

---

provided the owners with a monopoly through which players have been denied the rights enjoyed by employees in every other industry. Continuing Congress' past inaction on this issue would be tragic.... Since Justice Blackmun rendered that court's opinion [in 1922], baseball's antitrust exemption has paved the way for seven work stoppages to occur, and presented with a chance to act, Congress has balked each time. The season may be over, but the opportunity for Congress to act is not. I urge all Members, of course, to fully support this effort by Congressman Williams, but I think we should go further and I urge all Members of Congress to support the efforts going forward in the Judiciary Committee to finally cure this problem once and for all by taking away the antitrust exemption from baseball.[39]

Taking a different tack, other subcommittee members suggested that the baseball strike did not warrant congressional involvement, and that it should be resolved through collective bargaining. Excerpts from the statements of Representatives Peter Hoekstra, Steve Gunderson, and Harris W. Fawell, respectively, are as follows:

> I would encourage Congress at this point in time to stay out of this situation. I would encourage the witnesses to go back to the bargaining table to solve their problems. If we are going to get involved, we should wait until after this strike is solved, and we should not do anything in a short period of time. We have much more pressing problems to deal with.[40] [Hoekstra]

> As a Republican and a State legislator, I joined with the labor movement in Wisconsin to support binding arbitration, mandatory binding arbitration to eliminate the possibility of a work stoppage among the public schoolteachers in our State. I believe there was clearly a national interest or at least a State interest that required us to do that, and in that context we then had to look at an alternative to resolving the labor disputes. My question, very frankly, is to what degree and how do we determine whether there is a similar national interest with America's pastime, and if so, then what ought to be the conditions for an alternative remedy?.... As I indicated earlier, I am not one who is philosophically opposed to the concept of binding public arbitration when there is an overriding public interest. My question to the players or to your representative is, because you seem to be the supporters of this legislation, what is the overriding public interest which would compel the United States Congress to order final and binding arbitration in this situation?[41] [Gunderson]

> I generally agree with the Chairman in not believing that we should mandate settlements. I think that probably as rough as this may be, it should be allowed to play out, and who knows what the next chapter of baseball may be. "[42] "I speak as somebody who has played ball all my life, I love the game, it is fascinating, but I don't believe in the final analysis it is an economic tragedy in this Nation.... I basically take the view that we ought not to break into this collective bargaining process as long as it is there. Antitrust laws are not involved anyway.... The strike has got to be settled, I believe, by the players, by the owners getting together and recognizing that each has some trust and some basis to their stands.[43] [Fawell]

At least two of the subcommittee members who supported the imposition of binding arbitration raised yet another issue: the possible financial impact of the strike on stadium or team employees. Representative Martinez stated that the work stoppage was "an economic disaster to the people

---

[39] Ibid., pp. 3-4.

[40] Ibid., p. 117.

[41] Ibid., pp. 2-3, 115.

[42] Ibid., pp. 5-6.

[43] Ibid., p. 6.

who make a living from baseball.... [T]he people that sell the peanuts in the stands, the beer, and the people that work in the concessions."[44] Echoing Representative Martinez's concern, Representative Engel noted that "[t]housands of people, many of them my constituents, rely on Major League Baseball for their livelihood. They are the ticket takers, hot dog vendors, and small business owners in the community."[45]

Hearing on Baseball's Antitrust Exemption and the Strike (103rd Congress)

In September 1994, the House Committee on the Judiciary, Subcommittee on Economic and Commercial Law held a hearing on Major League Baseball's antitrust exemption and its relationship to the ongoing strike.[46]

As shown by the following passages, Representative Jack Brooks, chairman of the subcommittee, linked the two issues—baseball's antitrust exemption and the strike—and concluded that legislation was necessary.

> Now, Congress doesn't serve the function of mediator who shuttles between private parties to resolve individual disputes. But we are, however, policymakers, policymakers with a long memory.... They [the owners] may have shut it [baseball and the World Series, in particular] down for the first time since 1904, but you might be underestimating Congress' ability to respond to the debacle we have witnessed since August 12. They would be wise to remember there is a different rhythm to congressional deliberations and actions. The 406 games that have been lost, the 12.6 million people who have not enjoyed paying and going to a game have moved the issue of baseball's antitrust exemption to this committee's radar screen as never before.[47]

> As a result of the spectacle this Nation was forced to endure in the last few months and my very grave concerns for the future of the institution [baseball], I have come to the conclusion that legislation is needed to restore the principles of competition and fair play to the business of baseball. I am well aware that there may be insufficient time to pass a stand alone bill in the House before Congress adjourns, but I would remind the parties that the 104th Congress is schedule to convene well before spring training begins and well before the scheduled season opening on April 2. In addition, if before adjournment the Senate acts to attach a limited repeal of the exemption on other legislation and sends it to the House, I would be very open to allowing it to proceed directly to the President.[48]

Expressing similar sentiments, Representative John Conyers Jr. said: "We are not negotiators. We are not bargainers, but we do make the law. We are responsible for our antitrust law. And it seems to me that unless something happens before the end—the beginning of the season next year, I think Congress is going to have a very heavy obligation to move in one of these directions."[49]

---

[44] Ibid., p. 4.

[45] Ibid., p. 8.

[46] The subcommittee's initial hearing on baseball's antitrust exemption was held prior to the strike, on March 31, 1993.

[47] U.S. Congress, House Committee on the Judiciary, Subcommittee on Economic and Commercial Law, *Baseball's Antitrust Exemption (Part 2)*, 103rd Cong., 2nd sess., September 22, 1994, Serial No. 6 (Washington: GPO, 1994), p. 2.

[48] Ibid., p. 177.

[49] Ibid., pp. 153-154.

Representative Patricia Schroeder, in the following excerpt, characterized Congress's lack of action regarding baseball's antitrust exemption as implicitly creating a link between Congress and major league baseball.

> I have seen the polls that the owners are circulating that tell us the public does not favor Congressional involvement in the current dispute between the players and the owners. I would suggest that each year that Congress allows the [antitrust] exemption to stand is another year of Congressional involvement. By doing nothing, we are allowing the owners a special entitlement.[50]

Offering another, yet related, perspective, Representative Sherwood Boehlert talked of Congress's responsibility for professional baseball. He said: "We believe that because of the unique station that baseball holds in American society, and because of the legal privileges it has been granted by Congress, we have a special responsibility to ensure that the game endures."[51]

Although Representative Brooks concluded the hearing by citing the need for legislation, he and at least two other subcommittee members (Representatives Conyers and Hamilton Fish Jr.) encouraged the heads of the players union and Major League Baseball—both of whom testified at the hearing—to resolve their differences through collective bargaining. Their comments (Brooks, Fish, and Conyers, respectively) were as follows:

> You know, we deal with problems all the time up here where I may have this position, somebody else has another position, and we are hard set in them and we are going to go with them. Yet very often in Congress people get together and realize that there are third and fourth positions and what you thought was such a wonderful idea really is not that significant, that important, and that you could have been wrong. I could have been wrong. We could have done something else, and we reach those alternatives often here. That is what compromise is, that is what politics is all about. That is what negotiations are all about, and I would hope that you all would experience that opportunity. You have that opportunity any time.[52] [Brooks]

> I don't think anybody has missed the fact that the chairman and I would very much like the parties here to resolve this dispute themselves and get on with the game.[53] [Fish]

> Gentlemen, this has been an important hearing so far because it sounds like we might be able to get negotiations going again. I don't want to be overoptimistic, but I would certainly want to urge that if anything could come out of this hearing, the first thing that I think we would all rejoice about would be the fact that you were able to get back to the bargaining table, and I hope that could occur.[54] [Conyers]

---

[50] Ibid., p. 2.

[51] Ibid., p. 25.

[52] Ibid., pp. 148-149. Witnesses included the executive director of the Major League Baseball Players Association, Donald M. Fehr, and the chairman of the Executive Council of Major League Baseball, Allan H. "Bud" Selig. Hence, subcommittee members had an opportunity to address the parties to the dispute during the hearing.

[53] Ibid., p. 151.

[54] Ibid., p. 153.

H.R. 45, Baseball Fans and Communities Protection Act of 1995 (104th Congress)

In introducing H.R. 45, Representative Conyers identified baseball's antitrust exemption as being "at the root of the current strike," and suggested that Congress was in a position to intervene. Specifically, he said that "[w]e have the opportunity and ability to rescue the national pastime from its current dispiriting condition. Let's not allow this opportunity to pass by or be deferred. I urge all colleagues to join in the effort."[55]

H.R. 105, H.R. 106, H.R. 365, and H.R. 1612 (104th Congress)

In the absence of introductory statements or hearings, it is not known whether these bills were efforts to address the baseball strike, or reflect the Members' general interest in professional baseball. The bills and their titles and sponsors are as follows: H.R. 105, Baseball Antitrust Restoration Amendment of 1995, Representative Michael Bilirakis; H.R. 106,[56] Representative Michael Bilirakis; H.R. 365, Baseball Fans and Communities Protection Act of 1995, Representative Charles Schumer; and, H.R. 1612, Major League Baseball Antitrust Reform Act of 1995, Representative Jim Bunning.

H.R. 120, Baseball Fans and Communities Protection Act of 1995 (104th Congress)

Although he did not mention his bill specifically, Representative Bunning stated that "[m]ajor league baseball has to have this exemption removed for the good of the fans, the game, and anybody else that wants a season in 1995."[57]

H.R. 386, Professional Baseball Antitrust Reform Act of 1995 (104th Congress)

Similar to other Members who believed that the antitrust exemption was at the root of the strike, Representative James A. Traficant Jr. believed that "[r]emoving this [antitrust] exemption may be the only way to end the strike and save the 1995 season. That's why today I am introducing the Professional Baseball Antitrust Reform Act of 1995."[58]

H.R. 397, Major League Play Ball Act (104th Congress)

While proposing a partial, or complete, repeal of baseball's antitrust exemption was a relatively common response to the strike, Representative Pat Williams, in the following excerpt, recommended binding arbitration: "I have today introduced legislation to provide mandatory and binding arbitration if the parties fail to reach agreement. Collective bargaining in this country

---

[55] Rep. John Conyers, Jr., "Baseball Fans and Communities Protection Act of 1995," extension of remarks, *Congressional Record*, daily edition, January 5, 1995, p. E43.

[56] According to the Legislative Information System, this bill did not have a short title.

[57] Rep. Jim Bunning, "Major League Baseball," remarks in the House, *Congressional Record*, daily edition, January 17, 1995, p. H246.

[58] Rep. James A. Traficant, Jr., "Make Professional Baseball Subject to the Antitrust Laws," remarks in the House, *Congressional Record*, daily edition, January 5, 1995, p. E51.

works very well. The public, through their government, should intervene only in a crisis. We now have reached a crisis in the well-being of our national pastime."[59]

H.R. 735, National Commission on Professional Baseball Act of 1995 (104th Congress)

Representative John J. LaFalce, in discussing the rationale for his bill, noted that someone (that is, Congress) needed to protect the fans' interests, and proposed that regulating baseball was one way to do this. Excerpts from Representative LaFalce's statement are as follows:

> It is clear that baseball owners and players will continue to look out only for their own needs. But there is a crying need for someone to look out for the interests of fans, of taxpayers and of the communities in which both major league and minor league baseball is played. It is time for Congress to take steps to return baseball to the American people. The legislation I am introducing today seeks to accomplish this by creating an independent National Commission on Professional Baseball. The Commission would serve as a temporary regulatory body and impartial arbitrator to oversee the conduct of professional baseball until the legal status of major league baseball can be redefined either by negotiation or by congressional legislation.[60]

> My legislation does take the position that baseball's antitrust exemption is, in effect, a government-granted monopoly in much the same manner as a local public utility or transportation authority. And like any other publicly-sanctioned monopoly, my bill would require public oversight to assure that self-interest is not put above the interests of the public and consumers. In this regard, the proposed commission would be similar to the Federal Communications Commission, or any other public body with oversight over a restricted industry or market. An important difference, however is the fact that the authority of the proposed Commission is intended to be temporary during a period of deregulation of baseball from the current market restrictions imposed by baseball's current antitrust exemption. Since Federal law has permitted a restricted national market for major league baseball, the Federal Government has both the right and the responsibility to regulate this market, just as we regulate other monopolies, to assure that the public's interests are protected.[61]

H.R. 749[62] (104th Congress)

Advocating an approach also favored by several of his colleagues, Representative Estaban Edward Torres introduced legislation to repeal baseball's antitrust exemption. He provided the following reasons for doing so: "For the short term, I believe repealing the antitrust exemption will accelerate the end of the baseball shutdown, which threatens the livelihoods of thousands of Americans and the economies of cities and towns across the country. For the long term, I believe

---

[59] Rep. Pat Williams, "Play Ball," extension of remarks, *Congressional Record*, daily edition, January 5, 1995, pp. E49-E50.

[60] Rep. John J. LaFalce, "National Commission on Professional Baseball," remarks in the House, *Congressional Record*, daily edition, vol. 141, part 18 (January 30, 1995), p. E212.

[61] Ibid., p. E213.

[62] According to the Legislative Information System, this bill did not have a short title.

---

repealing the antitrust exemption will restore fairness to the fragile relationship of labor and management in professional baseball."[63]

H.R. 870 and S. 376, Major League Baseball Restoration Act (104th Congress)

As discussed below, President Clinton forwarded proposed legislation to Congress in 1995. His proposal became H.R. 870, which was introduced by Representative Pat Williams, and S. 376, which was introduced by Senator Edward M. Kennedy.

After noting that Congress generally prefers to let parties involved in labor disputes reach a settlement on their own, Senator Kennedy offered several reasons why it was desirable for Congress to intervene in the baseball strike. In the following excerpts from his remarks, he touched on Congress's authority to regulate interstate commerce and the special status of baseball in America.

> Generally, Congress is reluctant to inject itself in labor disputes. All of us hope that the parties will find a way to end the impasse and settle their differences voluntarily. But there are rare instances in which Congress has a role to play in settling such disputes, and this may well be one of those times.
>
> There is no doubt that Congress' constitutional authority to regulate interstate commerce gives us the power to enact legislation to settle this dispute. Many aspects of major league baseball affect commerce between the States....
>
> Obviously, Congress does not intervene in every labor dispute that burdens interstate commerce, but baseball is different and unique. It is more than a nationwide industry. It is our national sport. Baseball is part of American life.
>
> We in Congress as representatives of fans throughout the country should not remain silent while baseball is damaged by a strike that the owners and players seem unable to resolve themselves. Clearly, Congress has the power to act. The question is who speaks for Red Sox and millions of other fans across America. At this stage in the deadlock, if Congress does not speak for them, it may well be that no one will.
>
> For all these reasons, Congress can act and should be prepared to act. Legislation to end the strike would not set a precedent for injecting Congress into other labor disputes. There is still time for the owners and players to resolve this dispute on their own or to act voluntarily to establish a safety mechanism for doing so.[64]

S. 15, National Pastime Preservation Act of 1995 (104th Congress)

S. 15 was yet another bill that, if enacted, would have repealed baseball's antitrust exemption. Its sponsor, Senator Daniel Patrick Moynihan, made the following remarks when he introduced the bill:

---

[63] Rep. Estaban Edward Torres, "Legislation to Repeal Anti-Trust Exemption Regarding Major League Baseball," extension of remarks, *Congressional Record*, daily edition, January 31, 1995, p. E236.

[64] Sen. Edward M. Kennedy, "Binding Arbitration to Settle Baseball Strike," remarks in the Senate, *Congressional Record*, daily edition, February 9, 1995, p. S2430.

> As a result of this anomaly [baseball's antitrust exemption] in American law, Mr. President, the World Series was cancelled in 1994 for the first time since 1904. With none of the legal restraints that prevent other businesses from engaging in anticompetitive behavior, the baseball team owners are free to act as a cartel. To end this monopoly, Congress must remove baseball's antitrust exemption and subject the game to the same rules of law that apply to all other major league sports.... Many Members of Congress have begun to examine this issue more closely in view of the strike. My Friend Senator ORRIN HATCH, the new chairman of the Judiciary Committee, has indicated that he supports repealing the exemption and is prepared to move a bill quickly through his committee.[65]

S. 415, Professional Baseball Antitrust Reform Act of 1995, and S. 416, Major League Baseball Antitrust Reform Act of 1995[66] (104th Congress)

In February 1995, the Senate Committee on the Judiciary, Subcommittee on Antitrust, Business Rights, and Competition held a hearing on baseball's antitrust exemption and two bills, S. 415 and S. 416, that would apply antitrust laws to professional baseball. At the hearing, several Members offered diverse views regarding whether the proposed repeal of baseball's antitrust exemption ought to be linked to the strike and the desirability of congressional intervention in the strike.

Senator Strom Thurmond, who introduced S. 416, did not link the partial, or complete, repeal of baseball's antitrust exemption to the ongoing strike. The following are excerpts from his remarks:

> The Thurmond-Leahy legislation addresses baseball's antitrust exemption, but is not specially drafted in an attempt to solve the current baseball strike.... Some Members of Congress believe that we should not get involved during the current strike, while other Members have asserted that in the absence of a strike there is no need for the Congress to take action on this issue. Whether there is a strike or not, it is my belief that it is proper for the Congress to consider this antitrust issue as a matter of public policy.[67]

Regarding the purpose of the February 1995 hearing, Senator Thurmond said that it was "intended to focus on the policy implications of baseball's antitrust exemption, rather than the details of the current baseball strike and the course of the unsuccessful negotiations. Although the ongoing strike raises questions about the antitrust exemption, the problems in major league baseball go deeper than this one strike."[68] Senator Thurmond added that he "intend[ed] to continue working on this issue, even if the strike were to end today."[69]

Senator Thurmond also shared his thoughts on the circumstances under which it might be acceptable for government to intervene in a matter such as the baseball strike, indicating it

---

[65] Sen. Daniel Patrick Moynihan, "National Pastime Preservation Act," remarks in the Senate, *Congressional Record*, daily edition, January 4, 1995, p. S176. (Small capitals in original.)

[66] S. 415 and S. 416 are presented in a single subsection because one hearing was held for both bills.

[67] Sen. Strom Thurmond, "The Major League Baseball Antitrust Reform Act of 1995," remarks in the Senate, *Congressional Record*, daily edition, February 15, 1995, p. S2660.

[68] U.S. Congress, Senate Committee on the Judiciary, Subcommittee on Antitrust, Business Rights and Competition, *The Court-Imposed Major League Baseball Antitrust Exemption*, hearing on S. 415 and S. 416, 104th Cong., 1st sess., February 15, 1995, S. Hrg. 104-682 (Washington: GPO, 1996), p. 3.

[69] Ibid., pp. 2-3.

---

depended upon whether the public interest would be served. In the following passage, the Senator also commented on Congress's implicit involvement in baseball's antitrust exemption.

> Despite our interest in seeing the players return to the field, we must be ever mindful of the need to limit Federal Government intervention into matters best left to private remedies. The Congress should determine how much Federal involvement, if any, serves the public interest in this area. But as long as the special antitrust exemption remains in place for baseball, the Congress is involved. The Congress has an impact on the sport by simply permitting the special exemption to remain long after the factual basis for it has disappeared.[70]

Senator Orrin G. Hatch, who introduced S. 415, was one of several subcommittee members that linked the ongoing baseball strike to professional baseball's antitrust exemption, and, accordingly, supported eliminating the exemption. Senator Hatch's comments were as follows:

> Unlike other legislation that has been proposed, my bill would not impose a big-government solution. On the contrary, it would get government out of the way by eliminating a serious Government-made obstacle [baseball's antitrust exemption] to settlement....
>
> A limited repeal of this antitrust immunity is now in order. Labor negotiations between owners and players are impeded by the fact that baseball players, unlike all other workers, have no resort under the law if the baseball owners act in a manner that would, in the absence of the immunity, violate the antitrust laws. This aberration in the antitrust laws has handed the owners a huge club that gives them unique leverage in bargaining and discourages them from accepting reasonable terms. This is an aberration that Government has created, and it is an aberration that Government should fix....
>
> This legislation would not impose any terms of settlement on the disputing parties, nor would it require that they reach a settlement. Rather, it would simply remove a serious impediment to settlement—an impediment that is the product of an aberration in our antitrust laws. In short, far from involving any governmental intrusion into the pending baseball dispute, the legislation would get Government out of the way.[71]

Although Senator Patrick Leahy was Senator Thurmond's cosponsor, he is one of the Members who asserted that the antitrust exemption played a role in the strike. However, he also identified, in the following comments, two other factors that he asserted contributed to the ongoing dispute.

> There is a public interest in the resumption of true, major league baseball. The current situation derives at least in part from circumstances in which the Federal antitrust laws have not applied, Congress has provided no regulatory framework to protect the public, and the major leagues have chosen to operate without a strong, independent commissioner who could look out for the best interest of baseball. Thus, competing financial interests continue to clash, with no resolution in sight.[72]

Senator Daniel Patrick Moynihan, although an original cosponsor of S. 415, favored resolution of the labor-management dispute through collective agreement. Excerpts from his remarks are as follows:

---

[70] Ibid., p. 1.

[71] Sen. Orrin Hatch, "The Professional Baseball Antitrust Reform Act of 1995," remarks in the Senate, *Congressional Record*, daily edition, February 14, 1995, p. S2659.

[72] Sen. Patrick Leahy, "The Major League Baseball Antitrust Reform Act of 1995," remarks in the Senate, *Congressional Record*, daily edition, February 15, 1995, p. S2661.

Clearly baseball is a business engaged in interstate commerce, and should be subject to the antitrust laws to the same extent that all other businesses are. But the greater point is that the strike must be settled through good-faith bargaining between the parties. I will support this and any other effort that will move the parties forward toward a collective bargaining agreement—and the resumption of baseball in America as soon as possible.[73]

As a former Assistant Secretary of Labor under Presidents Kennedy and Johnson, I agree with Senator Hatch, Senator Kassebaum, and others who have said Congress ought not interfere in the collective bargaining process—in baseball or any other industry. Absent some compelling national interest, Congress has always been reluctant to intervene in labor disputes, and properly so. Yet by our *inaction* with regard to the antitrust exemption, we *have* been interfering with baseball for half a century.[74]

Other members of the subcommittee offered reasons why Congress should refrain from intervening in the strike. Senator Arlen Specter simply stated that he did not "think that the Congress ought to intervene when a dispute is in process, and certainly not to order binding arbitration."[75] Senator Howell Heflin, who said he had "great reservations about Congress intervening in any labor dispute," described two of them in the following passage:

Reservations, No. 1, as to whether or not we are equipped to be the decisionmaker and whether we ought to take action which might be favorable or unfavorable to one side or the other. I have also questions as to whether or not in any labor dispute anything other than the economic pressures that come to bear should have a substantial interest or controlling interest in the determination of the settlement of the dispute or the terms that come up. On the other hand, I want to see baseball played. I want to see the fans' interest in it gratified.[76]

Raising questions regarding, for example, Congress's priorities and the expected effectiveness of the proposed legislation, Senator Nancy Landon Kassebaum said the following:

At the outset, let me say that I believe it would be a mistake for Congress to intervene in the current dispute between the Major League Baseball owners and players. It is not the role of Congress—absent a national emergency—to force a settlement or take sides in a private labor dispute. To make an exception in this case would establish a very dangerous precedent.... Let me outline briefly my three principal objections to the Hatch-Moynihan bill.

First, the Hatch-Moynihan bill [S. 415]—by its own terms—would be a direct intervention by Congress in the current baseball labor dispute.... Again, I believe it is a mistake for us to intervene by changing the rules in the middle of the game.

Second, not only would Hatch-Moynihan intervene in the current dispute, it would, worse still, take sides.... Hatch-Moynihan would treat the baseball owners less favorably than any other industry by excluding baseball's collective bargaining process from federal antitrust laws. This would allow the players to take the dispute to court, a right nonlabor organization now enjoys....

---

[73] Sen. Daniel Patrick Moynihan, "The Professional Baseball Antitrust Reform Act of 1995," remarks in the Senate, *Congressional Record*, daily edition, February 15, 1995, p. S2660.

[74] U.S. Congress, Senate Committee on the Judiciary, Subcommittee on Antitrust, Business Rights and Competition, *The Court-Imposed Major League Baseball Antitrust Exemption*, p. 7. (Italics in original.)

[75] Ibid., p. 73.

[76] Ibid., p. 68.

Finally, it is my view that consideration of this or any legislation, at this time, will only impede further negotiations and decrease the likelihood of a settlement. As long as one side or the other believes there is a possibility that Congress will step in, meaningful negotiations will not occur.[77]

S. 627, Major League Baseball Antitrust Reform Act of 1995 (104th Congress)

Having introduced S. 415 previously, Senator Hatch, along with four colleagues, including Senator Thurmond, introduced a new bill, S. 627, in March 1995. Senator Hatch's and Senator Thurmond's positions remained unchanged regarding whether the purpose of the legislation was to facilitate the resolution of the strike (Hatch's position), or to terminate Congress's connection to baseball's antitrust exemption (Thurmond's position).[78]

During a hearing on S. 627, several members of the Senate Committee on the Judiciary provided a variety of reasons why Congress ought not to intervene in the strike. Questions about congressional priorities, the potential for legislation to disrupt collective bargaining efforts, and concern that congressional action would be viewed as favoring one party to the dispute over the other were put forth as reasons for Congress not to act. Senator Specter's, Senator Paul Simon's, and Senators Hank Brown and Dianne Feinstein's comments were as follows, respectively:

> Whatever the merits of eliminating major league baseball's broad, judicially created exemption from the antitrust laws, Congress should not act while the labor situation remains uncertain. Any action we take is certain to be viewed as favoring one side to the dispute or the other. In such instances, Congress acts best when it does not act at all. The complex labor problems that have characterized baseball for the past years ought to be resolved by the parties without congressional interference.... Whether or not that [baseball's] exemption ought to be retained, I believe strongly that given the current state of play, it would be a mistake for Congress to enact this bill. This bill would only upset the current situation, making it less likely that the parties to baseball's labor strife will be able to resolve their dispute between themselves. We should not lose sight of the fact that voluntary collective bargaining is the basis of labor relations in this country. The parties should be left to settle their current impasse themselves without interference from Congress.[79] [Specter]

> In approving a repeal of major league baseball's longstanding antitrust exemption, this Committee has decided to alter the balance of power in an ongoing labor dispute between millionaires while the truly pressing problems facing our nation remain unresolved. Congress should be devoting its time and resources to other matters rather than inserting itself into a controversy for which both sides deserve blame. Indeed, of the many labor disputes ongoing in America today, I can think of few, if any, that are less deserving of our attention than this one.... The variety of problems facing our professional sports leagues demonstrates that even if professional baseball is a deserving subject of Congress's attention, such consideration should not take place on an *ad hoc* basis, in response to one 'crisis' or another, but should be part of an overall and careful reexamination of professional sports under the law. Only by studying the issue raised by S. 627 in this broader context can Congress avoid the justifiable

---

[77] Ibid., p. 6.

[78] Sen. Orrin Hatch, "Major League Baseball Antitrust Reform Act," remarks in the Senate, *Congressional Record*, daily edition, March 27, 1995, p. S4660; Sen. Strom Thurmond, "Major League Baseball Antitrust Reform Act," remarks in the Senate, *Congressional Record*, daily edition, March 27, 1995, p. S4660.

[79] U.S. Congress, Senate Committee on the Judiciary, *Major League Baseball Reform Act of 1995*, report to accompany S. 627, 104th Cong., 2nd sess., February 6, 1006, S.Rept. 104-231 (Washington:GPO, 1996), pp. 19-20.

criticism that it is simply playing favorites in a rancorous dispute that, but for the parties' stubbornness and lack of reason, should have been resolved long ago.[80] [Simon]

The current bill intervenes in a continuing labor dispute. The majority report justifies this legislation on the basis that it 'would help resolve baseball's labor problems.' This conclusion is dubious at best. The middle of an ongoing labor dispute is not the right time to change the rules of the game. Both President Clinton and his chosen mediator, William Usery, repeatedly stated that the problems of baseball should be decided at the negotiating table. But, every time this issue comes before Congress, the parties drop what they are doing, leave the negotiating table, and focus their efforts on legislation.[81] Proponents of the legislation suggest that all of the labor discord in Baseball can somehow be attributed to the existence of the exemption and that its elimination would be a labor panacea. Nothing could be further from the truth. In fact, all that its elimination would cause is unbridled litigation.[82] [Brown and Feinstein]

White House Efforts to Aid in Resolving the Strike

On October 14, 1994, the Secretary of Labor, Robert Reich, announced that former Labor Secretary William Usery had "agreed to mediate the labor dispute between Major League Baseball players and owners. And the players and owners have agreed to resume negotiations with Bill Usery as special mediator."[83]

On January 26, 1995, President Clinton issued a statement, saying that he had asked Mr. Usery "to bring the owners and the players back to the table, and to step up the pace and intensity of his mediation efforts. I have asked him to report back to me by February 6 with the progress they have made." While the President said that "[i]t has always been my belief—and continues to be— that the baseball strike, like any labor dispute, should be settled through good-faith bargaining between the parties," he added "[b]ut we cannot wait indefinitely."[84]

On February 7, 1995, President Clinton "summoned the two sides to the White House ... for a last-ditch negotiating session," which, ultimately, was unsuccessful.[85] Speaking in the briefing room at the White House shortly before 11:00 p.m. on February 7, President Clinton provided the following update:

> Clearly they are not capable of settling this strike without an umpire. So I have now concluded, since I have no legal authority in this situation, as all of you know and have known for some time, that I should send to the Congress legislation seeking binding arbitration of the baseball dispute. This is not a request for a congressionally imposed

[80] Ibid., pp. 21-22. (Italics in original.)

[81] Ibid., pp. 24-25.

[82] Ibid., p. 26.

[83] White House, "Press Briefing by Secretary of Labor Bob Reich, Bill Usery, Bud Selig, and Don Fehr," press release, October 14, 1994, http://clinton6.nara.gov/1994/10/1994-10-14-briefing-on-baseball-negotiations.html.

[84] U.S. President (Clinton), "Statement on the Baseball Strike," *Weekly Compilation of Presidential Documents*, vol. 31 (January 26, 1995), p. 124.

[85] David Hosansky, "President Swings and Misses at Baseball Strike," *Congressional Quarterly*, February 11, 1995, p. 449.

solution. It is a request for the only process we have left to us to find a solution through neutral parties.[86]

After acknowledging that Congress has "other pressing business," the President added, "[a]t least when the bill [I propose] goes to the Congress, the American people can make themselves heard one way or the other on the legislation and Congress can consider it."[87]

The next day, President Clinton transmitted proposed legislation, "Major League Baseball Restoration Act," to Congress. As discussed above, Representative Williams and Senator Kennedy introduced the bill in the House of Representatives (H.R. 870) and the Senate (S. 376), respectively. The President's rationale for proposing legislation included the following reasons: "If the dispute is permitted to continue, there is likely to be substantial economic damage to the cities and communities in which major league franchises are located and to the communities that host spring training. The ongoing dispute also threatens further serious harm to an important national institution."[88]

2011 National Football League Lockout

The National Football League's previous collective bargaining agreement took effect on March 8, 2006, and was to expire on the "last day of the 2012 League Year."[89] As described in the following excerpt from the CBA, however, either party to the agreement could opt to terminate it prior to the established expiration date:

> *Section 3.* **Termination Prior to Expiration Date:**
>
> (a) Either the NFLPA [NFL Players Association] or the Management Council may terminate both of the final two Capped Years (2010 and 2011) by giving written notice to the other on or before November 8, 2008. In that event, the 2010 League Year would be the Final League Year, and the Agreement would continue in full force and effect until the last day of that League Year, except for the provisions related to the Draft, which would expire as prescribed in Article XVI, Section 1 [of the CBA].[90]

In May 2008, NFL team owners voted unanimously to opt out of the CBA and negotiate a new agreement for the 2011 season and subsequent seasons.[91] Following unsuccessful efforts by the

---

[86] U.S. President (Clinton), "Remarks on the Major League Baseball Strike and an Exchange with Reporters," *Weekly Compilation of Presidential Documents*, vol. 31 (February 7, 1995), p. 204.

[87] Ibid., p. 205.

[88] U.S. President (Clinton), "Message to the Congress Transmitting the 'Major League Baseball Restoration Act,'" *Weekly Compilation of Presidential Documents*, vol. 31 (February 9, 1995), p. 224.

[89] National Football League, NFL Management Council and NFL Players Association, *NFL Collective Bargaining Agreement 2006-2012*, March 8, 2006, p. 240. A "league year" is "the period from March 1 of one year through and including the last day of February of the following year, or such other one year period to which the NFL and the NFLPA may agree." (Ibid., p. 4.)

[90] Ibid., p. 240. (Boldface and italics in original.) "'Capped Year' means any League Year for which a Salary Cap is in effect." (Ibid., p. 6.) "'Salary Cap' means the absolute maximum amount of Salary that each Club may pay or be obligated to pay or provide to players or Player Affiliates, or may pay or be obligated to pay to third parties at the request of and for the benefit of Players or Player Affiliates, at any time during a particular League Year, in accordance with the Rules set forth in Article XXIV (Guaranteed League-wide Salary, Salary Cap & Minimum Team Salary) [of the CBA], if applicable." (Ibid., p. 7.)

[91] National Football League, "NFL Owners Opt Out of CBA," news release, at http://www.nfl.com/news/story?id= (continued...)

---

league and the union to negotiate a new agreement, both parties accepted, in February 2011, an invitation from the director of the Federal Mediation and Conciliation Service (FMCS) to mediate their dispute. Seventeen days of mediation took place, between February 17 and March 11, under the auspices of the FMCS. On March 11, the FMCS issued a press release stating that the agency's director and deputy director had determined that "no useful purpose would be served by requesting the parties to continue the mediation process at this time."[92] On March 11, the NFLPA notified the NFL that it had "decertified," and the following day the NFL announced that it was imposing a lockout.[93] Following additional negotiations, the NFL and NFLPA announced, at a joint press conference on July 25, 2011, that the two parties had reached an agreement.[94] During that same week, team facilities were opened to players and training camp began. The first preseason games are scheduled for August 11-15.[95]

Congressional Response

Table 8 shows the legislative measure that was introduced in response to the lockout.

(...continued)

09000d5d80868b78&template=without-video&confirm=true. In announcing that the owners voted to opt out of the current CBA, the NFL stated that "[t]he current labor agreement does not adequately recognize the costs of generating the revenues of which the players receive the largest share; nor does the agreement recognize that those costs have increased substantially—and at an ever increasing rate—in recent years during a difficult economic climate in our country. As a result, under the terms of the current agreement, the clubs' incentive to invest in the game is threatened. There are substantial other elements of the deal that simply are not working. For example, as interpreted by the courts, the current CBA effectively prohibits the clubs from recouping bonuses paid to players who subsequently breach their player contracts or refuse to perform.... Our objective is to fix these problems in a new CBA." (Ibid.) As reported by the *Pittsburgh Tribune-Review*, DeMaurice Smith, the head of the NFLPA, said that "'[t]he players of the National Football League are still in the dark about why this deal [collective bargaining agreement] isn't good enough.... And the easiest way to demonstrate any problem with the deal is the way any business in American demonstrates it: They turn over what the profit or loss numbers are. And if there's a problem with the model, we'll fix it." (Scott Brown and Carl Prine, "Union Chief: NFL Headed for Lockout," *Pittsburgh Tribune-Review*, August 19, 2009, at http://www.pittsburghlive.com/x/pittsburghtrib/sports/steelers/s_638933.html.)

[92] Federal Mediation and Conciliation Service, "Statement by FMCS Director George H. Cohen on NFL-NFLPA Talks," news release, March 11, 2011, at http://www.fmcs.gov/assets/files/Public%20Affairs/2011%20Documents/Statement_on_NFL-NFLPA_Talks_3-11-2011.pdf.

[93] National Football League, "NFL Statement on 'Decertification'-Litigation-Lockout," press release, March 12, 2011, at http://www.nflmedia.com/wps/myportal/!ut/p/c1/hY5NC4JAGIR_0juutm5HK3aNLXVJS73IImKCHx0i6N-ndM5mjg8PM1TS3NG-utY-u2m0PeVU8koz13AZMggBCbZVkT4d9oDnzrzgFY-FOI8IZp74YE6m1S6VTGTOH_u27K37C8ePBFj1Y49TFE5DQwWVfqU9_v2h0ouDY2DURobGhQIVfdPa-k2PIUeX3M0HPIfc0g!!/dl2/d1/L0lJSkIna21BL0lKakFBTXlBQkVSQ0pBISEvWUZOQTFOSTUwLTVGd0EhIS83X0sONIE2RkgyMEdUUzEwSUFRRzVGSFEzMEcwX1dDTV9DT05URVhUPXdwcy93Y20vbXljb25uZWN0L05GTE1lZGlhL25mbCttZWRpYStzaXRlL25ld3MvbmZsK3N0YXRlbWVudCtvbitkZWNlcnRpZmljYXRpby1saXRpZ2F0aW9uLWxvY2tvdXQ!/?PC_7_K46Q6FH20GTS10IAQG5FHQ30G0_WCM_CONTEXT=/wps/wcm/myconnect/NFLMedia/nfl+media+site/news/nfl+statement+on+decertificatio n-litigation-lockout.

[94] National Football League, "NFL-NFLPA Press Conference Announcing 10-Year Agreement," July 25, 2011, at http://nfllabor.com/2011/07/25/nfl-nflpa-press-conference-transcript/.

[95] National Football League, "2011 National Football League Calendar," at http://nfllabor.files.wordpress.com/2011/07/2011nflcalendar.pdf.

Table 8. 112th Congress: Legislative Measure Related to the 2011 NFL Lockout

Legislative Measure	Brief Summary	Hearing Held or Written Report Published?	Number of Cosponsors	Final Major Action
H.R. 1060	Remove the sport of football from the Sports Broadcasting Act of 1961 (P.L. 87-331).a	No	0	Referred by the House Committee on the Judiciary to the Subcommittee on Intellectual Property, Competition and the Internet.

Source: Legislative Information System, at http://www.congress.gov.

Note:

a. Under the Sports Broadcasting Act of 1961, professional sports teams may pool their broadcasting rights when negotiating television deals. If this bill were enacted, NFL teams might not be permitted to continue to negotiate as a single entity when seeking television deals for broadcasting their games.

Upon introducing this bill, Representative John Conyers, Jr., stated that its purpose was to ensure that "a congressionally granted antitrust immunity is never again misused to build up an improper 'war chest' to gain leverage in a football lockout...."[96] According to Representative Conyers, when the NFL had negotiated its television contracts in 2008, the league had "insisted on provisions that would shield it from the economic impact of a lockout."[97]

Discussion

As measured by the number of legislative measures introduced and hearings held, and as shown in **Table 9**, Congress was most active during the 1994 strike. The 232-day baseball strike lasted much longer than the two NFL strikes and included the loss of the 1994 World Series. The 1982 and 1987 strikes were relatively short by comparison, lasting 57 days and 24 days, respectively. Although the 1987 strike involved the use of replacement players for several games during the regular season, the season was capped by the Super Bowl. The 1982 Super Bowl also was held.

Table 9. Congressional Activity During Strikes

	1982 NFL Strike	1987 NFL Strike	1994 MLB Strike	2011 NFL Lockout
Legislative Measure(s)	3	1	22a	1

---

[96] Rep. John Conyers, Jr., "The Prevent Lockout of Athletes This Year Act," extension of remarks, *Congressional Record*, daily edition, March 14, 2011, p. E478.

[97] Ibid. ESPN summarized the dispute over television revenue as follows: "The union accused the NFL of failing to secure the maximum revenue possible when it restructured broadcast contracts in 2009 and 2010, and claimed the deals were designed to guarantee owners enough money to survive a lockout. The union argued this violated an agreement between the sides that says the NFL must make good-faith efforts to maximize revenue for players." (Associated Press, "Federal Judge Rules NFL Violated Deal," ESPN, March 2, 2011, at http://espn.go.com/espn/print?id=6172379&type=story#.)

	1982 NFL Strike	1987 NFL Strike	1994 MLB Strike	2011 NFL Lockout
Hearing(s)	0	0	5	0

Source: Legislative Information System, at http://www.congress.gov.

Notes:

a. As discussed above, it is uncertain whether H.R. 105, H.R. 106, H.R. 365, and H.R. 1612, which are included here, were related to the 1994 MLB strike.

Table 10 organizes the legislative measures according to the method proposed for resolving the dispute. S. 3003 (97th Congress) is included in two columns (impose binding arbitration and require league and players to resume activities) because it included two noteworthy provisions.

Table 10. Methods Proposed for Resolving the Strikes

Support Reconciliation (Congress)	Establish a Commission (Congress)	Impose Binding Arbitration (Congress)	Eliminate or Modify MLB's Antitrust Exemption (Congress)	Amend the Sports Broadcasting Act (Congress)	Require League and Players to Resume Activities (Congress)
H.Res. 597 (97th)	S. 2401 (103rd)	S. 3003 (97th)[a]	S. 2380 (103rd)	H.R. 105 (104th)[b]	S. 3003 (97th)[a,c]
H.Res. 598 (97th)	H.R. 735 (104th)	H.R. 5095 (103rd)	S.Amdt. 2601 to H.R. 4649 (103rd)	H.R. 1060 (112th)	
S.Res. 294 (100th)		H.R. 397 (104th)	H.R. 4965 (103rd)		
		Y.R. 870 (104th)	H.R. 4994 (103rd)		
		S. 376 (104th)	H.R. 45 (104th)		
			H.R. 106[b] (104th)		
			H.R. 120 (104th)		
			H.R. 365[b] (104th)		
			H.R. 386 (104th)		
			H.R. 749 (104th)		
			H.R. 1612[b] (104th)		
			S. 15 (104th)		
			S. 415 (104th)		
			S. 416 (104th)		
			S. 627 (104th)		

Source: Legislative Information System, at http://www.congress.gov.

Notes:

a. This bill is included in two columns.

b. As discussed above, it is uncertain whether H.R. 105, H.R. 106, H.R. 365, and H.R. 1612 were related to the 1994 MLB strike.

c. While urging the NFL and the NFLPA to "take all necessary steps to resume activities," S. 3003 would have directed them to return to the "status quo" that existed "prior to 12:01 antemeridian [morning] of September 21, 1982," which, in effect would have required that games be resumed. (Sec. 3 of S. 3003 (97th Congress).) The final game played before the strike began took place Monday night, Sept. 20, 1982, between the Green Bay Packers and the New York Giants. Hence, the language in S. 3003 refers to the status quo of the regular season. (Len Pasquarelli, "Lengthy Strike Has Mostly Been Forgotten," ESPN.com, Sept. 21, 2007, at http://sports.espn.go.com/nfl/columns/story?columnist=pasquarelli_len&id=3030311.)

Three methods were proposed for ending the 1982 or 1987 NFL strikes—impose binding arbitration, encourage the parties to reconcile their differences, or require the league and players to resume normal activities (that is, resume playing games). Neither of the latter two options was proposed for baseball. Major league baseball enjoys a unique status as the only professional sport in the United States that has a broad antitrust exemption, and 15 legislative measures targeted the exemption, attempting to eliminate or modify it. Four measures were introduced that would have imposed binding arbitration on baseball; two measures would have established a commission to oversee baseball; and one measure would have amended the Sports Broadcasting Act regarding professional baseball.

The following table shows the disposition of the legislative measures introduced or offered in response to the 1982 NFL strike, the 1987 NFL strike, the 1994 MLB strike, and the 2011 NFL lockout.

Table 11. Disposition of Legislative Measures

Withdrawn (Congress)	Not Reported by Committee[a] (Congress)	Placed on Senate or House Calendar (Congress)	Agreed to by Voice Vote (Congress)
S.Amdt. 2601 to H.R. 4649 (103rd)	H.Res. 597 (97th)	S. 2380 (103rd)	S.Res. 294 (100th)
	H.Res. 598 (97th)	H.R. 4994 (103rd)	
	S. 3003 (97th)	S. 376 (104th)	
	H.R. 4965 (103rd)	S. 627 (104th)	
	S. 2401 (103rd)		
	H.R. 5095 (103rd)		
	H.R. 45 (104th)		
	H.R. 105 (104th) [b]		
	H.R. 106 (104th) [b]		
	H.R. 120 (104th)		
	H.R. 365 (104th) [b]		
	H.R. 386 (104th)		
	H.R. 397 (104th)		
	H.R. 735 (104th)		
	H.R. 749 (104th)		
	H.R. 870 (104th)		
	H.R. 1612 (104th) [b]		
	S. 15 (104th)		
	S. 415 (104th)		
	S. 416 (104th)		
	H.R. 1060 (112th)[c]		

Source: Legislative Information System, at http://www.congress.gov.

Notes:

a. These are bills that were referred to a committee, but were not reported by the committee. See **Table 5**, **Table 6**, and **Table 7**.

b.   As discussed above, it is uncertain whether H.R. 105, H.R. 106, H.R. 365, and H.R. 1612 were related to the 1994 MLB strike.

c.   This bill, which was introduced early during the first session of the 112th Congress, may yet be reported out of committee at some later date. However, on July 25, 2011, the NFL and the NFLPA announced that they had reached an agreement, which effectively ended the 2011 NFL lockout. (National Football League, "NFL-NFLPA Press Conference Announcing 10-Year Agreement," July 25, 2011, at http://nfllabor.com/2011/07/25/nfl-nflpa-press-conference-transcript/.)

Among the 26 legislative measures introduced, the only one that was approved was S.Res. 294 (100th Congress), which encouraged NFL players and management to return to the bargaining table. Four bills, all related to the 1994 baseball strike, were placed on a Senate or House calendar. The one amendment (S.Amdt. 2601 to H.R. 4649 (103rd Congress)) that was offered was withdrawn. Most of the measures (20) were not reported by committee.

Appendix A. Summary of NFL Labor History[98]

Chronology

1982	"The NFLPA's request to team owners to receive 55 percent of league revenue is denied, prompting a 57-day strike. The PA [players association] gains little."
1987	"NFL players vote to strike and owners field replacement players, After only 24 days, the players end their strike with no appreciable gains earned. The union files suit against the NFL, claiming that labor laws and collective bargaining, as conducted by the league, aren't working for the benefit of its players. A judge agrees, and in 1989, the Plan B limited system of free agency begins."
1989	"A federal appeals court reverses the 1987 court decision, claiming that antitrust laws do not apply because the NFLPA is a labor union. NFLPA Executive Director Gene Upshaw immediately decertifies the union."
1992	"Players win the right to free agency in the Freeman McNeil antitrust case, clearing the way for new collective-bargaining agreement negotiations."
1993	"The NFLPA is recertified as a union, the final step necessary before signing a new CBA. The new agreement establishes the league's first year of free agency and its first salary cap, which is set at $35 million. That cap will subsequently rise; for the 2009 season, it is projected to be $123 million."
2005	"The salary cap increases to $85.5 million, boosted by the opening of five new stadiums and three extensive renovations since the last extension of the CBA, in 2002."
2006	"NFL owners vote 30-2 to accept the NFLPA's proposal to extend the CBA, a deal that gives the players approximately 60 percent of total football revenue."
2008	"Owners in May vote 32-0 to opt out of the CBA they agreed to extend in 2006."
2011	In March, the NFL imposed a lockout, which was lifted in July as the league and the players reached an agreement on a new CBA.

---

[98] David Broughton, "NFL Labor Timeline," *Sports Business Journal*, September 1, 2008, p. 32.

Appendix B. Sports and Labor-Management Relations[99]

The National Labor Relations Act (NLRA)[100] governs labor-management relations in the private sector and applies generally to professional sports employers. Under the NLRA, employers and unions are required to bargain in good faith with respect to wages, hours, and other terms and conditions of employment.[101] Employers and unions are required to bargain over these mandatory subjects of bargaining to the point of impasse. The NLRA does not obligate either party, however, to agree to a proposal or to make a concession.[102] In fact, collective bargaining presupposes the availability of certain economic weapons as part of the negotiating process.[103] For example, employees are permitted to strike if collective bargaining fails to achieve higher wages or improved working conditions.[104] Similarly, during certain work stoppages, an employer may use replacement workers to continue the operation of its business.

Although the NLRA contemplates possible strikes by employees, it does provide for mediation and conciliation services to settle certain disputes. The NLRA authorizes the Federal Mediation and Conciliation Service (FMCS) to provide mediation and conciliation services upon its own motion or upon the request of one or more of the parties to a dispute whenever "in its judgment such dispute threatens to cause a substantial interruption of commerce."[105] The FMCS is directed, however, to avoid mediating disputes that would have only a minor effect on interstate commerce, if state or other conciliation services are available to the parties.[106] Where the FMCS is involved in a dispute, it is limited to providing only mediation and conciliation services, and may not issue a binding arbitration decision.

As noted earlier in this report, numerous measures were introduced in Congress in 1982 and 1994 to prescribe binding arbitration to resolve the NFL and MLB strikes. In general, these measures would have established a board or panel to take testimony, conduct hearings, and review relevant books and records. The board or panel would then consider various factors in conjunction with the information it received before rendering a final decision or agreement that would bind the parties and replace the expired collective bargaining agreement. Some of the factors that would have been considered include the history of collective bargaining agreements between the parties, the changes in circumstances of the parties, and an owner's ability to pay.[107] Unlike recent legislation, such as the Employee Free Choice Act,[108] that would have amended the NLRA to prescribe binding arbitration if certain conditions are not met in any private labor negotiation,

---

[99] This section was written by Jon Shimabukuro, Legislative Attorney, American Law Division.

[100] 29 U.S.C. §151 *et seq.*

[101] 29 U.S.C. §158(d).

[102] *Id.*

[103] *See* The Developing Labor Law 1572 (John E. Higgins, Jr. et al. eds., 2006).

[104] 29 U.S.C. §163.

[105] 29 U.S.C. §173(b).

[106] *Id.*

[107] *See, e.g.,* Major League Play Ball Act, H.R. 5095, 103ᵈ Cong. (1994); Major League Baseball Restoration Act, H.R. 870, 104ᵗʰ Cong. (1995).

[108] For additional information on the Employee Free Choice Act, see CRS Report RS21887, *The Employee Free Choice Act*, by Jon O. Shimabukuro.

many of the NFL and MLB measures would have established a panel or board to resolve a specific strike. It appears that the panel or board would have ceased to operate once a decision was reached.

Arbitration is often favored by disputing parties because it allows generally for the selection of arbitrators who have expertise in the industry in which the dispute arises.[109] Unlike judges who may or may not be familiar with certain industry concepts, arbitrators may be people who have worked as officials or regulators in the relevant community.[110] Indeed, at least one of the MLB measures would have established an arbitration board consisting of one representative of the owners of major league baseball selected by the owners, one representative of the major league baseball player's association selected by the association, and a third individual selected in accordance with the procedures of the American Arbitration Association or procedures otherwise agreed to by the parties.[111]

Supporters of arbitration have also maintained that it provides for faster dispute resolution because it is not subject generally to the rules and procedures that exist with litigation. Increasingly, however, the use of lawyers is becoming more common in arbitration. Consequently, whether arbitration is really a cost-effective alternative to litigation has been questioned. It has also been noted that arbitration fees may be costly.

---

[109] *See, e.g.,* Jay J. Madrid & Jay G. Martin, Advantages of Using Mediation and Arbitration to Settle Environmental Disputes, *in* Environmental Dispute Resolution: An Anthology of Practical Solutions 46 (Ann L. MacNaughton & Jay G. Martin eds., 2002).

[110] *Id.*

[111] *See* Major League Play Ball Act, H.R. 5095, 103ᵈ Cong. (1994).

Appendix C. Antitrust Exemptions Applicable to Professional Sports[112]

There is one statutory exemption from the antitrust laws applicable generally to professional sports, the Sports Broadcasting Act,[113] and two non-statutory exemptions: the so-called "baseball antitrust exemption" describes the fact that major league baseball, alone among professional sports, is not covered by the antitrust laws;[114] the judicially created labor-antitrust exemption is utilized by all professional sports leagues inasmuch as it is applicable to the collective bargaining agreements between players and their teams. Each will be briefly summarized in the following paragraphs, after which an element in many, if not most, professional team-sports contracts—the "reserve" clause[115]—will be noted and briefly discussed. Finally, there will be a short section on the 1998 congressional attempt to limit the "baseball antitrust exemption." Further, or more specific, information may be obtained directly from the author(s).

Sports Broadcasting Act (SBA)

The SBA's five sections include the following:

The first section of the act (15 U.S.C. §1291) authorizes professional sports teams (including football teams) to pool, by "joint agreement," their broadcasting ("sponsored telecasting")[116] rights in their games in order that their leagues may sell or transfer those rights; and specifically makes the federal antitrust laws inapplicable to such joint agreements and sales or transfers.[117] (In 1988, the U.S. Court of Appeals for the Second Circuit ruled that the provision does not limit the antitrust exemption to a single, pooled-rights contract with a single television network.[118])

15 U.S.C. Section 1292 clarifies that the antitrust exemption granted in Section 1291 does not apply to contracts for the sale of telecasting rights that seek to limit the buyer's right to telecast

---

[112] This section originally was written by Janice E. Rubin, who has retired from CRS. Readers with questions about this section's subject matter may contact Kathleen Ann Ruane.

[113] 15 U.S.C. §§1291-1295 (P.L. 87-331).

[114] For more information on Major League Baseball's antitrust status, *see* CRS Report 98-820, *"Curt Flood Act of 1998": Application of Federal Antitrust Laws to Major League Baseball Players*, by Janice E. Rubin. Rubin. The Report also addresses the interaction between the two non-statutory exemptions/doctrines.

[115] The similar clause in NFL contracts is called the Rozelle Rule.

[116] The exemption does not apply to agreements between the leagues and cable or satellite media. Shaw v. Dallas Cowboys Football Club, Ltd., 1998 WL 419765 (E.D. Pa. 1998), *aff'd.*, 172 F.3d 299, 301 (3d Cir. 1999). According to the court of appeals, after it noted some of the act's legislative history, SBA's purpose was "to preserve the availability of [professional] games on *free* broadcast" (emphasis added).

[117] The section was amended in 1966 to permit the merger of the then-American Football League (AFL) and the NFL on the condition that the merger increase rather than decrease the number of professional football teams.

[118] U.S. Football League v. National Football League, 842 F.2d 1335, 1353 (2d Cir. 1988), *aff'g*, 644 F.Supp. 1040 (S.D.N.Y. 1986). Although multiple contracts *are* considered to be covered by §1291, those which seek to limit the rights of individual teams to sell their rights to games not included in a contract remain fully subject to the antitrust laws to the extent that they attempt to impose such limits (*e.g.*, Chicago Professional Sports Ltd. Partnership v. National Basketball Ass'n, 754 F.Supp. 1336, 1352 (N.D. Ill. 1991), *aff'd*, 961 F.2d 667 (7th Cir. 1992), *reh. denied; cert. denied*, 506 U.S. 954 (1992)).

games into *any* territory, except that a league may prohibit the telecasting of games into the home territory of any team when that team is playing a home game.[119]

The other three sections of the SBA (1) carve out Friday evenings (after 6 o'clock) and all day Saturdays between the second Friday in September and the second Saturday in December for high school and college games by specifically noting that the antitrust exemption provided in Section 1291 does not apply to contracts that permit the telecasts of professional games during those times *if* the high school or college games were announced prior to August 1 of the applicable year as "regularly scheduled for such day and place" (§1293); (2) clarify that with the exception of the exemption granted in Section 1291, the applicability of the antitrust laws to "organized professional team sports" remains unchanged (§1294); and (3) define "persons" as meaning individuals, partnerships, corporations, or "unincorporated association[s][120] or any combination" of them (§1295).

"Baseball Antitrust Exemption"

The so-called "baseball antitrust exemption"—a convenient and much-used shorthand phrase—is, technically, not accurate because it implies positive action by Congress to grant an exemption. In fact, the "exemption" is the result of an historical accident: the first case to come before the Supreme Court alleging a violation of the antitrust laws occurred prior to the Supreme Court's expansive interpretation of the Commerce Clause. In that case, the Court held that the business of putting on "exhibitions of baseball" could not be considered commerce for purposes of federal antitrust jurisdiction;[121] and although the Court has had several opportunities to reverse its position that the antitrust laws are not applicable to professional baseball, it has never done so, preferring that the change be made specifically by Congress.[122]

---

[119] The prohibition is applicable to agreements with any station whose broadcast signal penetrates into the home territory, not only those actually located in the home territory. *See, e.g.*, WTWV, Inc. v. National Football League, 678 F.2d 142 (11th Cir. 1982).

The 1973 legislation (an amendment to the Communications Act) that required the leagues to lift the blackout of any pooled telecast if all the tickets available for purchase five days before the game were sold seventy-two hours prior to the game (47 U.S.C. §331) was repealed in 1975, as mandated in the law, P.L. 93-107. The leagues have continued, however, to abide by that regime: "The sports leagues, wary about angering legions of sports fans who have become accustomed to watching sold-out home games on television, have, in effect, made the law permanent by voluntarily adhering to its terms for the past sixteen years. Few people, in fact, realize that the legislation expired at the end of the 1975 football season." (Dean A. Rosen, BACK TO THE FUTURE AGAIN: AN OBLIQUE LOOK AT THE SPORTS BROADCASTING ACT OF 1961, 13 (NO. 5) Entertainment L. Rep. 3, 6 (1991)).

[120] "The NFL is an unincorporated association of football teams ...." Stringer v. National Football League, 474 F.Supp.2d 894, 898 (S.D. Ohio 2007); *see also*, other cases in which the NFL is a party, including, *e.g.*, National Football League Players Ass'n v. National Football League Properties, Inc., 1991 WL 156280 (S.D.N.Y. 1991).

[121] Federal Baseball Club of Baltimore, Inc. v. National League of Professional Baseball Clubs, 259 U.S. 200, 208-209 (1922). The suit against the National League alleged it had acted in contravention of the antitrust laws to destroy the rival Federal League.

[122] In 1953, in Toolson v. New York Yankees, Inc. 346 U.S. 356, 357, the Court reaffirmed the position it had taken in Federal Baseball, although it did note that "if there are evils in this field which now warrant application to it of the antitrust laws it should be by legislation" and not by judicial action. By 1972, although the Court's "expanding interpretation of the commerce power" led it to state unequivocally that "professional baseball *is* a business ... engaged in interstate commerce," and despite the fact that in 1972 it considered the antitrust exempt status of professional baseball to be an "anomaly" and an "aberration," the "inconsistency or illogic" of the situation would have to be "remedied by the Congress and not by the Supreme Court" (Flood v. Kuhn, 407 U.S. 258, 282, 284, emphasis added; *see, also*, Piazza v. Major League Baseball, 831 F.Supp. 435 (E.D. Pa. 1993)).

While the fact of an antitrust exemption for professional baseball has been recognized since 1922, the *extent* and *scope* of that exemption, however, has been the subject of some lower court discussion. At least one court has interpreted the Supreme Court's holdings and language as limiting the exemption to baseball's "reserve system," noted, *infra,* pursuant to which player movement from team to team may be restrained.

Labor-Antitrust Exemption

The judicially created labor-antitrust exemption holds that Congress's desire to foster collective bargaining is best furthered by permitting employees who wish to jointly negotiate the terms of their employment contracts to do so without fear of violating the antitrust laws. The exemption is not completely open-ended, however, specifying that the practices negotiated must (1) inherently constitute mandatory subjects of collective bargaining (i.e., be bona fide terms or conditions of employment); (2) be no more restrictive than necessary to realize the goal(s) it/they purport(s) to achieve; and (3) be embodied in a valid, genuinely negotiated (i.e., arm's-length) collective bargaining agreement. In addition, some courts have indicated that another factor to be evaluated is whether the restraint embodied in the agreement affects only or primarily the parties to the agreement (as opposed to competitors of either).[123] If the labor-antitrust doctrine is applicable, it covers the management as well as labor parties to a collective bargaining agreement. As the Supreme Court explained in *Connell Construction Co. v. Plumbers & Steamfitters Local Union No. 100,*

> The nonstatutory exemption has its source in the strong labor policy favoring the association of employees to eliminate competition over wages and working conditions. Union success in organizing workers and standardizing wages ultimately will affect price competition among employers, but the goals of federal labor law could never be achieved if this effect on business competition were held a violation of the antitrust laws. The Court therefore has acknowledged that labor policy requires tolerance for the lessening of business competition based on differences in wages and working conditions.[124]

The "Reserve" Clause in Professional Sports; Congress's Attempt to Address the Issue in the Context of the "Baseball Antitrust Exemption"

Under most circumstances, the value of an offered service (e.g., the services of a professional athlete) would be determined by the market. Prospective buyers of that service would bid on it and bargain with the seller, who, if he has an especially unique or valuable commodity to sell, would profit from his ability to exploit the competition among potential buyers. Once a professional athlete is under contract to a sports team, however, the "reserve" clause in professional sports prohibits that interplay among market participants by, in essence, binding the athlete to the team that has him under contract—at least in the year following the contract's

---

[123] *See, e.g.,* Mackey v. National Football League, 543 F.2d 606 (8th Cir. 1976); Smith v. Pro-Football, Inc., 593 F.2d 1173 (1978); Connell Construction Co. v. Plumbers & Steamfitters Union, 421 U.S. 616 (1975).

[124] 421 U.S. 616, 622 (1975).

expiration. The argument that "the restriction of competition for players' services is not a type of restraint proscribed by the Sherman Act" has been made and rejected.[125]

But that same court would not dismiss the utility of the NFL's "Rozelle" rule, noting that the "'ostensible purposes' of the rule are to maintain competitive balance among ... teams and protect the clubs' investment in scouting, selecting and developing players."[126] Even the district court hearing the relatively recent challenge to baseball's "reserve" clause observed:

> Clearly the preponderance of credible proof does not favor elimination of the reserve clause. With the sole exception of plaintiff [Curt Flood] himself, it shows that even plaintiff's witnesses do not contend that it is wholly undesirable; in fact they regard substantial portions meritorious.[127]

Thus, the various "reserve" clauses have not been struck down completely; they have, however, been modified to conform to judicial criticism of their enforcement and/or lack of bona fide bargaining—most "reserve" clauses are simply imported from the leagues' constitutions and bylaws and inserted in their standard player contracts.

In the years after the Supreme Court's *Flood* decision[128] refusing to alter or remove baseball's antitrust exemption, Congress had made several attempts to act on the Court's invitation in that case to correct the historical accident of baseball's antitrust exemption,[129] but none was successful until the passage of the Curt Flood Act by the 105th Congress.[130] The Curt Flood Act is applicable

---

[125] *Mackey, supra,* note 12, 543 F.2d at 616-17.

[126] *Id.* at 611.

[127] Flood v. Kuhn, 316 F.Supp. 271, 275-76 (S.D.N.Y.1970).

[128] Flood v. Kuhn, 407 U.S. 258 (1972).

[129] "The Court has expressed concern [over the years, in several prior opinions] about the confusion and the retroactivity problems that inevitably would result with a judicial overturning of Federal Baseball [Club of Baltimore, Inc. v. National League of Professional Baseball Clubs, 259 U.S. 200 (1922)]. It has voiced a preference that if any change is to be made, it come by legislative action that, by its nature, is only prospective in operation. ... The Court [has] noted ... that the slate with respect to baseball is not clean. Indeed, it has not been clean for half a century. ... This emphasis and this concern are still with us. We continue to be loath, 50 years after Federal Baseball and almost two decades after Toolson [v. New York Yankees, Inc. 346 U.S. 356 (1953)], to overturn those cases judicially when Congress, by its positive inaction, has allowed those decisions to stand for so long and, far beyond mere inference and implication, has clearly evinced a desire not to disapprove them legislatively. Accordingly, we adhere once again to Federal Baseball and Toolson and to their application to professional baseball. ... *If there is any inconsistency or illogic in all this, it is an inconsistency and illogic of long standing that is to be remedied by the Congress and not by this Court.*" 407 U.S. at 283-284 (emphasis added).

[130] P.L. 105-297, codified at 15 U.S.C. §26b. Its predecessor history includes, for example, the Final Report of the House Select Committee on Professional Sports (94th Congress), which had concluded that "adequate justification does not exist for baseball's special exemption from the antitrust laws ... [and] the exemption should be removed in the context of overall sports antitrust reform" (*Inquiry into Professional Sports* (January 3, 1977) at 60). Among the first responses to that conclusion was H.R. 2129, prompted, according to its sponsor, by both the Court's and the Committee Report's "invitations" to Congress; H.R. 2129 would have legislatively "repealed" the entirety of baseball's antitrust exemption (*i.e.*, made the antitrust laws applicable to professional baseball), not merely the exemption as it has been applied to the "reserve" clause. *See* 125 CONG. REC. 2521 (February 13, 1979).

In the 103d Congress, several bills to end or limit the exemption either remained pending in House and Senate Committees or were reported but not acted upon by either the full House or Senate. For a more detailed listing of the bills, *see* CRS Report 98-820, *"Curt Flood Act of 1998": Application of Federal Antitrust Laws to Major League Baseball Players,* by Janice E. Rubin.

In the 104th Congress, which was energized by the 1994 strike, more than a dozen measures to either make the antitrust laws unqualifiedly and generally applicable to professional baseball, or applicable only to specific issues (*e.g.*, player-
(continued...)

---

to major league baseball players,[131] clarifying that they are covered by the antitrust laws in transactions concerning their employment to the same extent as are other professional athletes.[132] Among the issues specifically not covered or affected (in addition to employment relations with minor league players) is "the agreement [known as the 'Professional Baseball Agreement'] between organized professional major league baseball teams and the National Association of Professional Baseball Leagues."

We are not aware of any litigation brought pursuant to the Curt Flood Act: although the act does get major league professional baseball players past the courthouse door by denying their employers the "we're-not-covered-by-the-antitrust-laws-so-this-case-must-be-dismissed" argument, as the foregoing material has indicated. Once in court many professional athletes have been frustrated in their attempts to challenge practices they consider onerous if those practices are embodied in valid collective bargaining agreements. The Curt Flood Act neither prevents the courts from recognizing the nonstatutory labor-antitrust exemption, nor provides guidance on the interpretation of that exemption.

Author Contact Information

L. Elaine Halchin, Coordinator
Specialist in American National Government
ehalchin@crs.loc.gov, 7-0646

Justin Murray
Information Research Specialist
jmurray@crs.loc.gov, 7-4092

Jon O. Shimabukuro
Legislative Attorney
jshimabukuro@crs.loc.gov, 7-7990

Kathleen Ann Ruane
Legislative Attorney
kruane@crs.loc.gov, 7-9135

(...continued)

management relations), were introduced but not acted upon.

[131] But explicitly *not* to minor league players pursuant to 15 U.S.C. §§26b(b) and 26b(b)(1), which state that "No court shall rely on the enactment of this section as a basis for changing the application of the antitrust laws ... any conduct, acts, practices, or agreements [concerning] the business of organized professional baseball relating to or affecting employment to play baseball at the minor league level," and specifically not to "any reserve clause as applied to minor league players."

[132] 15 U.S.C. §26b(a).